# NEVER SAY ALWAYS:

# PERSPECTIVES ON
# SAFETY BELT USE

by

J.Peter Rothe and Peter J. Cooper

363.125
R84n

Published in the United States by:  Transaction Publishers
Rutgers - The State University
New Brunswick, New Jersey 08903

**Canadian Cataloguing in Publication Data**

Rothe, John Peter, 1948–
     Never Say Always


     Bibliography: p.
     ISBN 0-88738-775-6

1. Automobiles – British Columbia – Seat belts – Attitudes 2. Automobiles – British Columbia – Seat belts – Psychological aspects I. Cooper, P.J. II. Insurance Corporation of British Columbia III. Title

TL242.R67  1988            363.1'2572'09711            C88-092095-5
TP

# PREFACE

Recent years have witnessed profound efforts to have motorists use safety belts. To a great extent such persuasions have succeeded, but a significant portion of the motoring public still resist the challenge.

There is no conspiracy involved. Individuals have perceptions of reality which are shaped by particular cultural, social, technological and economic events. This, at its broadest level, is what the safety belt debate is about.

We are nowadays more familiar with notions of driving risk than at any time since the advent of automobile use. The mass penetration of official messages has brought the sights and sounds of safety belt wearing directly into our living rooms, courtrooms, schools and workplace lunchrooms. They have become, so to speak, part of the background noise of contemporary life.

Why, for many, only noise and nothing more? Presentations of official views on safety belt wearing can be unconvincing because of their concern for "what should be" without consideration of "what is." Research, educational program development, and policy efforts have concentrated on a world of reconstruction. Official statistics, formal logic, traditional empirical research designs, and technological perspectives of an ideal or uniform motoring society have been used to represent people's lives in a rapidly changing world. Sensitivity to people's beliefs, traditions, unquestioned rules of social conduct, and other realities of daily life has been left out of the discussion.

"What is happening in people's lives" seems to us to be a question whose answers are full of promise. Rather than bombard people with a formal version of "what is," it is time to articulate "what really is," and rework the answers into worthwhile critiques that people can accept without a loss of face. To do that we need a new set of lenses, a new series of assumptions. What makes this book different is its focus on what ordinary people think about safety belts as distinct from what experts tell them they should think.

We undertook the modest task of exploring principles of life that animate people's thinking about wearing safety belts and that influence their behaviors. The notion that "the good driver wears safety belts and the bad driver does not" is challenged.

While it may be true that many of those who actively flout restraint use legislation have less than acceptable driving attitudes and behaviors, nevertheless both good and bad drivers alike have legitimate reasons for non-use stemming from a variety of driving situations.

Our challenge is based on responses gathered in intensive interviewing sessions with all kinds of motorists all over the province. To get at the depths of belief, we asked, listened, agreed and argued. In addition we brought to bear relevant data from roadside surveys, accident records and large scale safety belt campaigns. The combination of data sources enabled us to describe in depth not only people's broad social, cultural, political and philosophical beliefs but also more subtle processes of thought and personal meanings. These we believe are at the root of not wearing safety belts. They serve as reasons whereby motorists almost "never say always" to safety belt wearing.

This book has been written in an informative rather than a rigorously scientific style. Such a distinction will be most obvious in the chapters dealing with numerical data analysis where we have sacrificed a good deal of technical detail and terminology in the interest of improved comprehension for a broad audience. Those readers with a scientific or technical background will no doubt find such treatments lacking in the usually accepted depth of description but we trust they will accept our assurances that the methodologies employed were selected and undertaken in appropriate empirical manner.

# ACKNOWLEDGEMENTS

This book is different—different in a positive way. The degree of difference is a reflection on the support we were able to mount from a variety of competent and committed colleagues.

Interviews with groups of randomly-selected motorists throughout British Columbia, interviews with students at the University of British Columbia and biographical accounts written by other students were co-ordinated by Dr. Ken Stoddart of the Department of Anthropology and Sociology, University of British Columbia. Roadside observations and follow-up interviews were managed by Paul Roer of McLaren Plansearch Corporation. Safety belt wearing campaign evaluations were undertaken by Mary Cooper of British Columbia Research. The searching of driver record information was done by the staff of the British Columbia Motor Vehicle Department under the direction of June Byers and Janice Schmidt. Dr. Frank Navin of the University of British Columbia directed the study on vehicle speeds and damage.

We owe a special debt of gratitude to Mario Pinili who spent countless hours arranging and rearranging accident data on the computer, to Sylvia Fockler for coding open-ended responses suitable for data entry, to Lorna Olson for entering data into the computer, and to Byng Leong for editing the manuscript. We are also grateful to a group of "hidden" experts, without whom we would be lost—the hardworking members of the word processing department. To all, a special thanks.

# TABLE OF CONTENTS

PAGE

**Early experiments in transportation**

# CHAPTER 1

# RISK CONCEPT

# Introduction

Learning more about safety belts has become a major topic of interest among traffic researchers, physicians, police officers, government officials, and others. The research literature is replete with statistical descriptions and discussions about safety belt wearing rates in different jurisdictions throughout the world. Interest has traditionally been guided by the significance of reported official wearing rates. We often read that a province in Canada has a wearing rate of, say, 75 percent. The generalization is based on observations taken at given points in time and at specific locations. This is the interpretation accepted by social researchers although not necessarily understood by all research consumers.

We can accept the general nature of such interpretation, but we must question the ontological conception of statements based upon it. First, if the safety belt wearing rate at specific observational periods and at select sites is 75 percent, it is doubtful that we can safely say that 75 percent of the people in the province are habitual safety belt wearers. The generalization is elusive. The people observed simply happened to be wearing safety belts at that time as implied by the metaphor, "official wearing rate." Another survey at a slightly different time and location might also find a generalized 75 percent wearing rate. However, some of the the people who were unrestrained in the first survey might be restrained in the second, and vice versa. We are therefore left with the question, what does a 75 percent safety belt wearing rate really mean or, perhaps more appropriately, what does it not mean?

First, it does not mean that 75 percent of the people wear safety belts whenever they are in a vehicle. Secondly, it does not mean that the same people also necessarily wear safety belts at another locale or at a strategically different time. The reason for these caveats is that **people seldom wear safety belts every time they are in a vehicle**. Depending on the situation, people will take risks in relation to a given set of circumstances, at a given time. This is especially true when the locations vary between highway sites and urban streets.

Generally speaking, people take certain risks because they strive for some benefit or personal compensation. A homeowner on a Sunday afternoon risks falling from a ladder because he wants to reach the eaves on the roof just beyond the reach of his fingertips. A saw operater risks having a finger or hand cut off by a circular saw because he wants to benefit by way of wages from the sale of a finished lumber product.

Thompson (1980) further clarified the relationship between risk and benefits, by suggesting that in some situations, exposure to risk itself brings individuals benefits. The author clarified that in such cases the exposure is bundled up with the risk. For example, motocross racers may get as much satisfaction from knowing that their sport entails the chance of a serious spill than from trying to win the race. However, it is not the spill that they value but the heightened intensity of the experience which comes from the exposure and the added challenge of keeping it from happening. In lay language such people thrive on an adrenalin rush. Many participants who enjoy high-risk adventures such as rockface climbing, hang gliding, or skydiving do not envision themselves as taking outrageous chances. Rather they prefer to see it as a grand stimulant—overcoming challenging situations.

In traditional traffic safety research, the phenomenon of risk has been apprehended, analyzed, and conceptualized in at least five major ways. Zaidel outlined the five cornerstone approaches:

1. Risk is a label for the accident involvement rate of any component of the transport system relative to a chosen exposure measure.
2. Risk is a characteristic of traffic situations or of roadway and environmental conditions. Common examples are: "speed variability," "roadside obstacles," "restricted sight distance," "adverse weather," and "sharp curve." The attribution of riskiness to such characteristics is often based on measures of accident rates (relative risk); at other times, it is a result of a logical, causal analysis or driver's and researcher's intuition.
3. Risk is a description of certain driving behaviors such as: "maintaining short headways," "driving at high speeds," "not stopping at a stop line," and "driving after alcohol consumption." Used in this sense, risk implies a conscious choice by the driver.
4. Risk-taking, risk-avoiding, or cautiousness are personal dispositions. It implies a personality characteristic that should be consistently reflected in a variety of situations across different times.
5. Risk is a societal cost associated with the use of transportation systems. It may be assessed by accident rates, economic indices such as actual safety investment, or insurance premiums (1985, p. 438).

In traffic safety research, risk is used in a parsimonious mode—clearly and operationally defined according to the conditions and situations involved. It is used as the descriptive substitute for the "statistical likelihood of accident involvement." From a review of the accident and risk literature, it is reasonable to say that risk focuses on such features as risk-taking, risk perception, and risk compensation. To elaborate on risk, intricate conceptual and theoretical spider webs have been woven. Each web's pattern was designed to help us better define risk situations and risk behaviors. One such theoretical web was constructed to explain the relationship between safety belt wearing and the probability of accident, injury or death. Such probability is defined as the odds that something is going to happen or that it is not going to happen if a person wears a safety belt.

# Social Use of Risk

To say that "the driver of that red pickup truck who is not wearing a safety belt is at risk" is to use the term "risk" in a manner conceptually different from saying that "driving without safety belts is risky." The first example looks to an explanation of events which is built on probability indices arrived at from empirical investigations and statistical manipulations. The second example looks to the familiar, an everyday use of risk that comes from broadly defined behaviors shared by members of society. The second definition has a broad, everyday scope to it, whereas the first usage has a narrow physiological and/or epidemiological sense to it.

In an everyday sense, risk has no linguistic or rigid empirical anchor. It is related to people's natural feelings and experiences concerning certain situations, events, behaviors, objects, or actions. Risk has become, in terms expressed by Hayakawa (1945), a dead metaphor. It has become a mainstay of people's regular vocabulary. Risk is a dramatic concept used for a variety of purposes and dissimilar situations. It has equivocal or multiple meanings. We readily accept a banker's account of "financial risk," a boxer's version of "physical risk," a stockbroker's clarification of "risk capital," or an adjuster's talk of "insurance risk." We display an infinite province of meaning when we speak about "risking it," "running a risk," "incurring a risk," or "being a poor or good risk." Throughout all these examples the meanings of risk are understood through reference to the pragmatic context.

In all the diverse contexts the use of the metaphor risk implies some chance of loss. The loss may be identified as immediate or remote, and have a specific or general value. Although not necessarily defined, the quantity or quality of the loss is often assumed to be understood by interactants. To illustrate: we regularly hear the weatherman speak of "high risk of rain," a mother talk about her son "risking life and limb," a job applicant speak about "risking everything to get the job" or "risking nothing," and a teacher discuss a student's behavior as "risking the future." Concerning the weather, the loss is unspoken. It is assumed to be the loss of sun or nice weather. Although it is not explicitly stated it is understood that sun is a preferred climatic condition. In the case of an individual risking life and limb, the loss may be exaggerated to portray seriousness without any clear definition of severity. When we talk about risking everything or risking the future, the potential of loss is judged to be great within a vast scope of our financial and career tracts. When a person colloquially defines risk as "nothing to lose," there is either an implicitly understood judgment within the context of a conversation that things are so bad already that nothing could be worse, or the risk is so small that any potential loss is negligible.

In social discourse, risk is seldom quantified. Its meaning is guided by the organization of daily practices. It is supported by practical actions and results. Outcomes where someone actually loses everything because of a job interview are rare. Thus such risk assessments are not calculated according to probability, variability, or complexity.

In research-oriented discourse, the concept of risk occurs in a technical context. It is an explanatory concept based on logical relations between or among propositions. Risk is an abstraction far removed from commonsense experience. It is defined and used as a parsimonious concept so that research can be replicated.

As can be seen, the social or commonsense version of risk has multiple meanings based on situational circumstances, whereas the empirical use of risk is rigidly defined to best rationalize driver behavior. We must, therefore, be clear that when we speak of average citizens not knowing about certain health risks we should not assume that they understand risk as intended by the researchers. For them risk has different connotative and denotative suggestions related to socially organized events.

# Risk and Safety Belt Wearing

Wearing safety belts is a form of self-protecting behavior. On the basis of this assumption some traffic safety researchers have made a conceptual leap. They have proposed that there is a strong probability that a driver's attitude toward risk is a determinant of safety belt wearing where such is not regulated by law. Their formulation was built on research by Morgan (1967) who concluded that safety belt wearers were more likely than non-wearers to avoid important life risks by taking actions such as having up-to-date hospital or medical insurance, taking needed immunizations, and maintaining adequate cash in bank accounts. For, according to Williams and Malfetti (1970), there are enough correlations between drivers' attitudes and driving records to conclude that people tend to "drive as they live."

Along similar lines, Fhaner and Hane (1973) and Hannah (1975) published papers in which they outlined relationships between lifestyle characteristics, risk, and safety belt wearing. A conclusion reached by these researchers was that safety belt non-wearers were more likely to smoke and less likely to have had recent medical checkups. Hannah reported the following relationships:

1. Non-users registered preference for an automatic system like airbags while users preferred an effort-producing protective system.
2. Non-users showed a greater tendency than did users to report smoking while driving and to select high cutoff points for safe driving with respect to number of miles and consumption of alcohol.
3. Non-users indicated that they would tend not to obey a law mandating the wearing of safety belts.

Unfortunately, the author failed to explore fully the meaning of the term "safety belt non-users" as related to everyday discourse. Are they consistent non-users or part-time non-users on the basis of changing situations, attitudes and circumstances? How do any of these possibilities relate to certain lifestyle variables that span people's lives? For as Durkheim wrote, the researcher ought:

> to refute resolutely the use of concepts originating outside of science for totally unscientific needs. He must emancipate himself from the fallacious ideas that dominate the mind of the layman; he must throw off, once and for all, the yoke of these empirical categories, which from long continued habit have become tyrannical (1952, p. 32).

Evans (1983), in his attempt to support the hypothesis that safety belt wearers are less likely to take driving risks than non-users, concluded that drivers who voluntarily used safety belts followed other vehicles at longer average headways than non-users. More important was the fact that safety belt users were less likely than non-users to follow other drivers at close, risky distances.

Safety belt use and risk have also been combined with outcomes. More specifically, probabilities of serious injuries or death have been tabulated based on a collection of statistical data on safety belt wearing, vehicle mass, and in-car position of occupant. In this case, risk is defined within a cognitive style that includes direct measurements of road use and restraint system variables. Firm rules and clearly agreed-upon criteria of analysis were employed.

A number of researchers have examined injury risk as a function of restraint use. In 1978, the German HUK VERBAND research group analyzed 15,000 car crashes with passenger injuries to establish an objective risk of injury and safety belt usage. After analyzing all the data, the authors concluded that current safety systems—irrespective of the sometimes careless ways of fastening the belt could help to:

- Avoid the occurrence of 40 percent of all injuries.
- Reduce the death rate with regard to car occupants by approximately 50 percent.

They also discussed the relationship between objective risk and physical outcomes:

> The injury risks indicated in the present study could be reduced decisively. Head injuries of the categories minor and moderate would be reduced for driver and front-seat occupant by roughly 75 percent. Moderately severe injuries to chest and abdomen are reduced 20 to 60 percent although the belt forces are dissipated in this body area. It is true that slightly more injuries to the cervical spine occur, which can be explained by the fact that the upper part of the body is held back by the belt and that the head describes a rotational movement; these injuries are, however, limited to the injury severity degrees "minor" and "moderate." The risk factor of serious/critical injury to the cervical spine, on the other hand, diminishes sharply. Injury frequency rates for injuries to arms and legs are reduced by approximately 60 percent when safety belts are used (1978, p. 23).

We should mention that more recent assessments in the United States of safety belt effectiveness suggest that injury and fatality reductions may be lower than the levels mentioned above (e.g., Evans, 1987).

For traffic safety researchers like those of the HUK VERBAND, Evans, and others, risk is a robust concept. It is an important empirical artifact that is operationalized within a technological reality. To provide a logic to the concept, researchers determine risk on a key presupposition. They assume that drivers are rational decisionmakers who soberly choose to minimize or optimize risk functions according to accurate understandings of credits and liabilities connected to driving decisions. Risk avoidance activities and favorable attitudes toward general safety laws therefore become important artifacts supporting the assumption that risk is based on rational decision making.

# Who Defines Risk and Safety Belt Wearing?

A variety of professionals constitute the group which has become the major guardian of the process of risk definition. Epidemiologists, psychologists, engineers and other traffic safety researchers as a collective have developed the "state of the art" for explaining driving risk. To provide a more powerful conceptual and practical front, driver behavior-defined risks such as safety belt non-wearing have been placed under the broad umbrella of health risk (Jessor, 1985). Safety belt non-wearing now finds itself in the company of smoking, problem drinking, illicit drug use, and promiscuous sexuality. These have been labeled as problems or health-compromising behaviors worthy of research, planning and follow-up action. The latter is often undertaken by government organizations who give shape to the reality of professionals' views of the world.

A question of note arises. Who is politically obligated to inform the public about risk behavior such as safety belt non-wearing? Governments increasingly take on the responsibility to inform, persuade or warn people about risk in terms of technical facts and reasoning. Various "expert" definitions of risk have penetrated the political realms. Simple examples occur when provincial or state governments consider raising the driving age to 18 or 19 and the drinking age to 21. Their proposals usually reflect the findings of major research bodies.

Based on rationalized versions of risk, governments attempt to shape people's perception of risk and safety belt wearing through public service announcements on television and radio, information distribution in print, formulation of policy toward policing, and development of laws and sanctions. Through this process, government agencies, peripheral organizations and public interest groups such as safety councils have spent considerable energy trying to mold an ambiguous concept like risk into a precise, finely-defined justification for safety belt wearing. In so doing they have sought to create a vision of safety belt wearing as a proper, factual, and rational deterrent to risky behavior. The underlying intent is to channel people's interpretation of risk away from the public sphere and towards the expert sphere.

In traffic safety, restraint wearing as a risk area is characterized at a general level by the interplay of the "expert" and "public" spheres (Covello et al., 1987). From the "expert" perspective, estimation of risk probability is a matter of technical-empirical knowledge which includes sophisticated measurement techniques and language sources. On the "public" side, the determination of risk acceptance is made through decision-making processes which reflect relevant situational, social, economic and political factors. The public and expert spheres are, by definition, different (Leiss and Krewski, 1987). The challenge is for the experts to detail their assessment of risk in a manner whereby the citizenry as a whole are better able to familiarize themselves with the expert presentations, to participate in a variety of forums to refine meanings, and to reassess the experts' conceptions to fall within the public sphere.

Reassessment does not include control of interpreting or stereotyping people's internalized structures of what is real. In 1977, the United States Department of Transportation did just that. The National Highway Traffic Safety Administration (NHTSA) pinpointed certain beliefs and reinterpreted them as "myths." Organizations like the Washington State Safety Restraint Coalition called them fairy tales. Here are some published "fairy tales" and responses:

**Fairy Tale:** It takes too much time and trouble to fasten my safety belt.

**Response:** Now there's a fairy tale that's an earful. In reality, fastening your safety belt may take some time and trouble—but not too much. It all depends on:

- how complex your belt is.
- how well you know how to use your belt.
- how difficult it is to find the belt ends.

That much time and trouble you can live with—if you want to live.

**Fairy Tale:** I don't need a safety belt when I'm traveling at low speeds or going on a short trip.

**Response:** You can't believe every story flying around these days. The truth is that all driving can be dangerous.
More than 80 percent of all accidents occur at speeds less than 40 mph. Fatalities involving non-belted occupants of cars have been recorded at as low as 12 mph. That's about the speed you'd be driving in a parking lot.
Three out of four accidents causing death occur within 25 miles of home. Belt up before driving to your shopping centre—just as you would for a long trip.

**Fairy Tale:** I might be saved if I'm thrown clear of the car in an accident.

**Response:** Rubbish! The fact is that your chances of being killed are almost 25 times greater if you're thrown from the car. The forces in a collision may be great enough to fling you as much as 150 feet—about 15 car lengths. Safety belts can keep you from:

- plunging through the windshield.
- being thrown out the door and hurtled through the air.
- scraping along the ground.
- being crushed by your own car.

In almost any collision, you're better off being held inside the car by safety belts.

The above examples portray quite clearly how people's commonsense beliefs and everyday assumptions become candidates for ridicule. A more sedate approach is advisable—one that allows people to retain faith in their world view, yet which steers them towards information that should be attended to. By doing so we do not look at people's beliefs as being false. On the contrary, the beliefs are so unconsciously and so widely and deeply accepted within society that the question of their truth never comes up. And, according to Postman et al. (1988), this accounts, in large measure, for the extraordinary resistance of beliefs to change. We should attempt to interrelate the relevance of empirical facts with the relevance of everyday life without labeling, or expressing value judgments that may degrade people's views of themselves.

## Experts Say "What Is" and Citizens Say "What Really Is"

"Reality" is what we take to be true. What we take to be true is what we believe. What we believe is based upon our perceptions. What we perceive depends upon what we look for. What we look for depends upon what we think. What we think depends upon what we perceive. What we perceive determines what we believe. What we believe determines what we take to be true. What we take to be true is our reality (Zukav, 1979, p. 310).

A great deal has been said and volumes have been written about reality. Much sociological research has been initiated to establish the great divide between the official or causal version of "what is" (expert) and the person's public or social version of "what really is" (Gusfield, 1981). As indicated earlier, the "official" and "public" perspectives of risk and safety belt wearing realities are worlds apart. The dissimilarity is not only normal but expected if we consider that the world is made up of multiple group realities. Each is significant in defining behavior. The point is that one reality should not bulldoze its perspective over another one. Realities are people's security blankets. They should be treated with maximum empathy and tact.

"What really is" relates to Zukav's (1979) quote. It is our seminal premise in this book. We are concerned with people's interpretation of, and involvement in, cultural patterns or socially-approved rules of behavior as they relate to risk and safety belts.

People who wear or do not wear safety belts are involved with a variety of formal and informal social organizations and institutions that structure the world around them. Government, media, educational systems, family, friends, professions and unions are but a few entities that influence us on what to see and do, and how to see and do it. They comprise a cultural system of meaning which makes sense of our behavior. People's realities, therefore, are not unorganized entities waiting to be discovered and redefined. Based on them, individuals do things for reasons—reasons which personify experience, personal meaning, self-image and self-perception. So the process of not wearing safety belts may quite easily be experienced by people as normal, natural or self-evident. It is not sensational, deviant or delinquent. Average citizens may choose not to wear safety belts and consider the decision to be obvious, legitimate, unproblematic, and devoid of ambiguity. They may reflect on their actions after safety officials announce alternative reasoning structures on safety belt non-wearing. However, a level of mistrust may easily develop between public and expert groups. A countering response, based on research, may not only create ambiguity in people's minds but it may also shake the embedded belief system—their perceptions, their thought processes and their personal behavioral comfort zones. As a result, they are more likely than not to discount points of view that contradict their embedded realities.

When safety belt wearing becomes the object of scrutiny and attention, traffic safety professionals should not rush blindly in and myopically give an official version which assumes the ultimate "what is." They need to remind themselves that their versions of reality are demonstrated on the basis of empirical facts. Gusfield sensed the danger:

> The "facts" . . . have not risen to the consciousness of observers as natural and self-evident experience. Implicit in their emergence is an organization of thought and of activities which has impelled some persons to be publicly accepted as legitimate and authoritative observers, to select certain avenues of concern, and to neglect others (1981, p. 30).

Facts are objective truths of public wisdom. When we speak about facts we speak about multiple realities. Facts may be derived from scientific knowledge, empirical investigations, philosophical deduction or from personal knowledge and experience, among other sources. The same data can be defined differently as facts by scholars, practitioners, and lay people. For each they comprise "reality."

The social and cultural definitions of safety belt wearing rest on belief systems which identify facts considered by members of society as "what really happens" in cars. The logical and deductive conceptions of safety belt wearing, on the other hand, depend on facts which are systematically and objectively arranged into an order of scientific understanding. They define "what happens" in cars. Two components and two versions of reality thus co-exist. When we combine "what is" with "what really is," a realistic description on safety belt wearing evolves. We are in a better position to recognize how people define circumstances that influence their safety belt wearing behavior. Also, we move away from the unproven and highly speculative concept of "safety belt wearers" (although continued use of this term may be made for practical considerations). Instead, we begin to explore the theme that to say "always" is uncharacteristically predictable. It denies us a naturalistic view of people's realities, in which they are intuitive, willful, free and uncertain. They do things routinely as others expect and social contexts or situations dictate. If one of those situations happens to be the time when they are observed, then they become one of a designated research category. Yet it may be one of these times that everyday rationality demands action different from the usual. Consequently, when speaking about safety belt wearing, we should "never say always."

This book draws on the never-say-always theme. After an extensive two-year research effort which included written accounts by safety belt wearers and non-wearers, group interviews, province-wide roadside surveys, roadside observations and interviews with recurring wearers and non-wearers, and an analysis of the British Columbia accident database, we have uprooted a series of taken-for-granted reasons that influence some people to buckle up and others who refuse to buckle up.

Our monograph is organized according to prominent themes that recurred in the research. The identification and depiction are constructed on the basis of how people envision reality and how their constructions relate to statistical evidence. A combination of the everyday—tied-in with the empirically reconstructed—provides us with a nicely articulated structure governed by the real world of shared values and norms; yet it is supported by an objective posture. In the publication, "Rethinking Young Drivers," Rothe wrote that:

. . . there are two profoundly different ways of knowing a thing. The first implies moving around the object; the second, entry into it. The first kind of knowledge may be said to stop at the relative; the second, in those cases where it is possible, to attain the absolute . . . . If a social phenomenon is envisioned as a box the existence of an inside is seen. With this recognition an outside comes to mind. Although different, the inside and outside are mutually dependent, for the existence of the inside presupposes the existence of an outside, and vice versa. Specifically, the inside consists of individuals' "Lebenswelt" (life world) whereas the outside consists of generalized understanding of human actions "Anschauung" (external world) (1987, pp. 38-39).

The conceptual clarification of relating the inside (public) and outside (expert) perspectives is called complementarity (Rothe, 1987). However, throughout this book we have not endeavored to spell out the details of complementarity or describe minutely each study under research protocol. Instead, we tried to retain a sense of participants' points of view to trace out their lines of reasoning as they constructed them. We wanted to dig out what is genuine in collective life. Whenever possible, we have related technical findings to people's points of view. This has not been done to discredit or bolster everyday rationality, rather it adds a necessary dimension—that of empirical description. The methodological accounts for each study are included in the appendices.

# CHAPTER 2

# GETTING IN THE HABIT

# Introduction

Once safety belt wearing becomes a habit, so a popular line of reasoning goes, the safety belt wearing rate will increase and the number of auto accident deaths and severe injuries will decrease. In addition, once the habit has been formed it will remain with no further need for reinforcement. Habit formation is the prototype for changing behavior. Researchers have used it as an explanatory category to account for safety belt wearing, and safety belt wearers have selected it to explain why they decided to buckle-up.

In Hannah's (1975) questionnaire survey of safety belt users and non-users, the author noted that safety consciousness and habit appeared to be prime factors accounting for use, while non-habit and inconvenience appeared to be the prime factors accounting for non-use. Heron (1975) found that people who had not defined themselves as habitual safety belt wearers felt that they would consistently wear one under a law.

Habit, as a major response category for safety belt use, made an impact on three separate Insurance Corporation of British Columbia province-wide surveys. In the 1982 survey, 12 percent of all observed safety belt wearers reported that habit was their reason for wearing safety belts. Habit was cited by 12 percent of vehicle occupants who defined themselves as always wearing, and 10 percent of those who sometimes buckled-up. Five years later (1987 surveys), these proportions increased to 15 percent and 13 percent, respectively.

It is interesting to note that expressions of habit were not readily forthcoming when safety belt non-users were asked "why they did not wear safety belts." This inconsistency may suggest that "habit" is an expedient response for people who use them.

Unfortunately there is little clarification as to what constitutes habit. It is left to stand alone as a catch-all verbal receptacle to explain safety belt wearing behavior. Habit is used as a semantic device without applicable referents, an orphan that has no home. To make sense of safety belt wearing and habit we must provide some form of support for habit so that it becomes a more confident explainer of behavior.

# Habitualized Actions

All of people's activities may be subject to habitualization. Any action that is repeated frequently becomes cast in a pattern, which can then be reproduced with an economy of effort (Berger and Luckmann, 1967). Habitualization further implies that certain behaviors transcend temporality in that they were done in the past, are being done now and will be repeated in the future. Each replication is accomplished in the same manner as before, and it takes the same economical effort.

Habitualized actions become embedded as routines in people's general stocks of knowledge. Individuals take such actions for granted. They are inertial. That is, people's orientations to judgments, deliberations and decisions remain rigidly predetermined. Habits free the individuals from the burden of making decisions time and time again. They make it unnecessary for drivers to define each trip anew, step by step, in terms of actions such as putting on safety belts.

# Habit and Authority

Authority is defined by Weber (1949) as a probability—namely, it is the probability that a law, order or directive will be obeyed by individuals in a group. In order for there to be an effect, people must become habituated to the exercise of authority. They then get into the habit of obeying specific commands (Berger and Berger, 1975).

Habit is an important factor in allowing governments to rule. It contributes to making behavior predictable. It may be an illusion to consider safety belt wearing as a habit, which is based on conscious decision-making reflecting ideals of right and wrong. Governments and other agencies set up, publicize and in many jurisdictions enforce predefined patterns of vehicle occupant conduct like safety belt wearing. No doubt many drivers will buckle-up repeatedly to the point where the act is habitualized, but it cannot necessarily be said that the drivers have chosen to wear safety belts as an internalized obligation. Rather, they may wear safety belts solely because they were **forced** into repeated wearing.

Habit as response to authority carries a routineness but with a conditional or questionable commitment. Habit as a response to a claim of worth or self-defined sense of right carries great commitment. It becomes part of everyday rationality—the seen-but-unnoticed background for living. This process must persist up to a point where changing conditions cannot alter the habits. The "this is how these things are done" attains a firmness in consciousness. It becomes the world (Berger and Luckman, 1967).

We should not believe that the habit of safety belt wearing is near the stage of unalterability. Too many people buckle-up on the basis of authority. They may consider it a habit, but it is a low-level committed routine.

Safety belt wearing is a potentially equivocal behavior. Its sense of specificity is not so much habit as it is a continual accomplishment within different contexts. Circumstances do much to alter safety belt wearing behavior. Members of society create and sustain a sense of appropriate behavior by displaying activities considered to be routine. Sometimes the routine activities negate the habit. This is another reason why we should respond to the question of safety belt wearing in terms of "never say always." For example, drivers are in the habit of signalling turns. However, in an emergency they may flash their lights and not signal as they make speedy turns. How an emergency is defined and dealt with may be considered routine by observers. But it may break a driver's habit.

Habits of safety belt wearing may be broken for purposes of consistency with social norms underlying friendship, community responsibilities and family peace; for convenience, relation to technology, subjective interpretation of danger, risk and safety; and for image of self and others. The construction of reasons people have for breaking potential safety belt wearing behavior, goes against their wearing safety belts at all times. We need to look towards social situations and contextual variables to account for the variance in safety belt wearing conduct. Our perspective gives additional weighting to the phrase, "it depends on the situation."

## Situation, Circumstances and Individuals

Ortega wrote, *"Yo soy yo y mi circumstancia"*—"I am myself and I am my circumstances" (1961). Life is composed of numerous situations. Each situation is made up of circumstances—the things that encompass us (Stern, 1971). For us to maintain ourselves, we must at every moment decide how to deal with the circumstances. It is this reality which philosophers often call "being-in-the-world."

To live is to choose among possibilities that circumstances offer. We are responsible for what we are. Choosing to do this or that is to affirm a value and it is this affirmation that makes for humanness (Sartre, 1946). It is our responsibility as human beings to choose the correct behavior within a given set of circumstances.

Because circumstances change, choices for behavior change. Habit, in its dictionary definition, means:

. . . a way of acting through repetition . . . implies doing unconsciously and often compulsively. Habit suggests a fixed attitude or usual state of mind (Webster's Ninth New Collegiate Dictionary).

But, to choose is human. Therefore for a driver to choose whether or not to buckle up is a situational behavior related to value and circumstances. Furthermore, to choose not to wear safety belts in some situations may be considered by those involved to be both proper and reasonable.

# CHAPTER 3

# CIRCUMSTANCES OF EXPOSURE

# Introduction

Psychologists consider habits to be frequently repeated behavioral responses that have become associated with particular situations. However, situations change as do circumstances. In traffic, drivers experience numerous different situations in terms of distance, duration and location of driving. Each of these situations brings with it driving circumstances for which people may choose not to buckle up. Our interviews with drivers who were generally not full-time wearers, sought to explore this ground.

# Distance and Duration of Trip

A popular driver position is that mishaps are unlikely to occur during brief exposure, whether measured in time or distance traveled. A series of drivers suggested that it is unlikely that everyone "always" wears safety belts "all the time." They were asked if they always buckle up, and if they do not, when and why do they not. One member responded in a way that many drivers felt. There are no definite times when she does not wear her restraint! Sometimes she "just doesn't" and sometimes she "forgets." If she had to be specific she would say that the "just don't" times are for short trips around town such as going to the store or picking up the children from school. She never considers buckling up when she drives four or five blocks to mail a letter or to pick up something at the corner store. "There's no traffic," she said, "It's all residential." A short trip in a residential section becomes the horizon against which driving is considered functional and safe. When asked if she thought residential streets were "safer" than commercial ones, the motorist replied "yes" without the least hesitation. "There's no doubt about it," agreed another person. He would not buckle up for a short trip in his own neighborhood. A third respondent supported his agreement with an example of going to a real-estate open house on the weekend:

> I started to put my safety belt on out of habit and then said, "what the hell" and didn't bother. Neither did my wife. What can happen in a few blocks?

Some people's outlooks of safety and distance of trip become the bedrock on which decisions are made. A popular point of view is that safety on residential streets is guaranteed by limited traffic and the likelihood of children being nearby. With youngsters in the vicinity, drivers are more likely to be careful—at least, so the reasoning goes.

In an interview session with five drivers:

> . . . a participant said he "usually" buckles up but didn't for a two-week period when he did his vacationing young son's newspaper route. "It would be too much hassle to take it off and put it on again every time I stopped," he said. "There are no cops around at that time of the morning anyway." "What about the possibility of an accident?" asked the interviewer. "There are no cars around either," was the reply.

> . . . another participant said that he "never" wore his safety belts when he went golfing very early on Saturday and Sunday mornings. For years he has driven across town to a certain golf course without "ever" buckling up. Now, he drives to a closer golf course—still unrestrained. His reasons were similar to those of his group colleague: no police, no traffic, no chance of an accident! The discussion leader asked the golfer to consider the possibility of a single-vehicle incident, particularly on the freeway. For example, there was always the chance of a mechanical failure or hitting a patch of early-morning black ice and going off the road. The golfer noted that his vehicle—a sports car, which he admittedly drives over the posted speed limit—is in good repair. Besides, he is a good driver and "able to handle whatever comes along!" He added that he had been driving for nearly forty years and had never had "anything like that happen." Furthermore, he's never had a "real accident" and doesn't expect to be involved in one. Another participant suggested that the golfer's "number" may be coming up. The golfer dismissed this, noting that being accident-free is more than a matter of luck.

There was a collective belief that the commonsense observations of city streets being safer than highways would be borne out by an analysis of accident sites. Such an analysis would show fewer crashes on residential streets than on major thoroughfares. Wearers and non-wearers alike would not feel guilty making an around-the-neighborhood trip unrestrained. All the drivers we spoke to had done it at one time or another, forming a script of consistency. "The other night in the pouring rain," said one:

> I drove down the street to pick up my daughter who was babysitting with a friend. There was no way I'd put my belt on for that.

According to the gentleman, his daughter did not buckle up for the return trip either. There was noticeable support for his decision. Others, too, could see "no point in it" for such an occasion.

To promote further discussion and gain greater insights into belief structures of drivers the investigator initiated encounters by creating a false impression of what is happening. He characterized himself as always wearing safety belts and always ensuring his passengers do as well. If that meant waiting while the passenger decides, then so be it.

He was repeatedly chided for assuming a morally superior position. In the attempt to expose him for his elevated stance, discussants exposed some of their beliefs about "normal non-use of safety belts." "What if you were just going to the store, four or five blocks away?" asked a participant. When the interviewer replied that he would "definitely" buckle up on such an occasion, the participant laughed and accused him of being less than truthful. "Nobody bothers for a short trip like that," he noted. Another discussant defended the researcher by stating that "there are probably lots of cautious people" who wear their safety belts all the time, "even when it's not really necessary." The tag, "even when it's not really necessary," illustrated the real value that the speaker placed on caution and always wearing a safety belt. Another driver emphatically noted that "there's cautious and there's **cautious**." He reasoned that sometimes the exercise of caution is foolish, for the occurrence of the event for which one prepares is unlikely to happen. The motorist illustrated his belief by describing a friend who has an unwarranted fear of germs that lurk in public bathrooms. "When he leaves, he opens the door with a paper towel," he said.

The point of the bathroom tale was that while harmful germs could be anywhere, chances are they are not. The risk of mishap may be similarly understood: While you could have an accident on the way to the store a few blocks away, chances are you would not. A schema of interpretation readily used by citizens is that wearing safety belts on a short journey symbolizes a person who worries too much about things that are unlikely to happen. In such a situation, buckling-up would be not so much habit as compulsive behavior.

Story telling followed. More specifically, a tale was told about a lady who had an accident within a few blocks of her home. "She was on her way to the store and somebody hit her at an intersection," the speaker described. The driver was not wearing her safety belt. But, more importantly to the speaker, the driver was not injured. The latter descriptor was intended to structure the speaker's disbelief in the safety functions of safety belts. Another member of the discussion group seized upon the story to document and elaborate his point on exposure and risk. "See," he said, "even if you do have an accident it'll probably be just a little one where you don't need safety belts anyway."

In order to develop a progressively normative dimension about location and risk of accident, focus groups throughout British Columbia were asked to discuss the issue of where serious accidents happen. Members' perspectives formed a collective character. With little deviation, respondents agreed that serious mishaps are most likely to occur on the highway—primarily because of speed. As one driver stated:

> If you're doing a hundred or more and you hit somebody or go off the road it's gotta be a serious accident.

The discussant's constructs of the "known" was purposefully challenged. The researcher proposed that city speeds are sufficient to result in a serious accident. There was no reluctance among interviewees to recognize the general believability of the statement. But, when odds come into play, the highway is more likely than a city street to produce serious crashes. One discussant generated an example. He witnessed a pedestrian accident in which an older woman was hit while crossing the street. The driver attempted to avoid hitting the lady. By so doing, the driver who was proceeding downhill, suddenly braked and lost control of the car, and ended up hitting both a tree and the pedestrian. Severe head injuries resulted because the driver was not wearing a safety belt. He was thrown around on impact.

The tale of woe did not produce agreement from the speaker's peers. One businessman interpreted the scenario to support his own beliefs. He devoted time to carefully explain that the accident previously described was in reality a rare event. He was convinced that "most" city accidents do not have such grave consequences. "Most of the city crashes," he said with serious import, "would be like the ones described earlier, no injury . . . no need for safety belts."

The attitude toward safety and length and location of trip had a strong attractiveness to it. For both usual safety belt wearers and usual non-wearers, the decision not to wear safety belts arose from their beliefs about commonsense exposure circumstances and the possibility of mishaps. So strong were people's views about exposure and distance traveled that even when the topic of conversation focused elsewhere, exposure was repeatedly volunteered as a theme. An illustration to demonstrate the grasp of a certain reality whereby exposure is used to reason through other topics, highlights our conclusion. After a lull in conversation, the researcher offered to discuss the topic, "Forgetting to fasten safety belts. What does one do in such an instance?" Reactions were as follows:

> "It depends how far you're going," said one person. "If you're just going for a few blocks, it's hardly worthwhile." Another interviewee added, "You wouldn't put them on if you were almost there, would you?" This participant told of driving all the way between two widely separated municipalities without wearing a safety belt. She noticed that she didn't have it on as she was about to leave the freeway for the shopping centre. "It was only a two-minute drive," she said, "so I just left it off."

Similar stories were shared. Everyone could tell tales of non-wearing based on forgetfulness. The "oversight" was always related to short-distance trips. In these instances, motorists were not specifically making decisions to fail to wear safety belts, but were allocating their time, energy and attention elsewhere.

Further proof of how dedicated participants are to their belief in decreased risk on short trips was demonstrated when the investigator introduced persuasive analogies to different groups of drivers. Drivers were asked whether they locked their houses when they were left unoccupied for short periods of time. The decision to lock a residence was subject to full agreement. A commonsense rule was that you lock your house whenever it is left unoccupied. But few people locked them when someone was home. Of interest is that not one of the over 100 motorists had ever experienced break-ins, either personally or on their street. Furthermore, only a few members knew of anyone who had been burglarized. Yet random knowledge on break-ins was freely shared. Conversations produced such interesting revelations as, for example, one lady's statement that she always locks her house, regardless of whether someone is home. She heard that burglars rob you in the daytime while you are working in the garden. She called these thieves "green-thumb burglars."

For further clarification, group members were asked why they bothered going to the trouble of locking their houses if, by their own admission, the chance of unauthorized entry was minimal. Articulation of whether drivers locked their unoccupied houses whenever they left for short periods of time, like a trip to the corner store, was sought. With one exception, all members locked their homes. The strength of belief behind such a decision was shown by a member who told of returning to her house because she had forgotten to lock the door. Her correction took a half-hour, twenty minutes longer than it took for the original trip to the store. A lady's colleague defended the decision by suggesting that:

> "You never know what's going to happen. Somebody could be watching your house." This participant told a story about his parents, whose unlocked house was burglarized while they were at the racetrack. "They knew their pattern," he said.

The rule of life maintained by the motorists was that "these days" extreme caution should be exercised with regard to securing your home. We should never risk a burglary by keeping our doors unlocked.

To stretch the socially-approved boundaries of risk pertaining to burglary and safety belt wearing, participants were asked why they felt secure not wearing safety belts for a brief period of time, and yet felt totally insecure about leaving their houses unlocked for a short time. The analogy was not well received. A clear sense of risk differences was evident. The likelihood of a break-in was judged to constitute a stronger and more real threat than the likelihood of a traffic mishap. Motorists were occasionally shocked or taken aback by the researcher's problematic stance on this self evident truth.

To better reconstruct individuals' versions of risk, a personal approach was taken by the researcher. He flatly stated that his family is very lax about locking the door to their house. As a joking overture, one of the men asked where the researcher lived, intimating if he is not careful, his house could get burglarized. Other members lectured and reprimanded the discussion leader, indicating that laxness is very foolish because "there are so many break-ins." The researcher skirted the warnings by clarifying that to worry about a burglary was ill founded because whenever the house was unoccupied, it was only for short periods, perhaps a couple of hours at most. Still the concept of real risk prevailed. "That's all it takes," said one interviewee. "They (thieves) can be in and out before you know it."

The inconsistency between securing a house and securing a body was the grist for interesting exchanges. The researcher queried why drivers were so fastidious about securing their residences when they were absent for a brief period but were so lackadaisical about securing themselves when they were going to be traveling on the road for a brief period. Over and over again motorists held firm to the commonsense notion that the odds of getting into a crash are so remote that it is senseless to worry about it. "Nothing's going to happen on a short trip," was the popular line.

The role of the media over many years in reporting and sensationalizing crime undoubtedly has contributed to people's perception of the risk of being victimized. If safety belt non-use risks were to be similarly emphasized, perhaps the participants in our interviews would revise their concepts.

The relationship between risk of mishap and exposure was not only endorsed by the people who defined themselves as non-wearers, but it was also widespread as the reason for occasional non-use by regular safety belt wearers. In a province-wide survey undertaken in 1983, 67 percent of 5,409 people who were surveyed at roadside checkpoints in British Columbia wore safety belts. For the 33 percent of the vehicle occupants who were observed not to be wearing safety belts, 82 percent said that they do wear safety belts, but did not do so at this particular time. The major reason was that they were on a "short trip." Similar findings were evident in the 1982 and 1985 surveys. Perhaps profession of regular safety belt wearing should carry a footnote, ". . . except for short trips."

More recently, in a 1987 provincial roadside survey of 4,390 occupants sponsored by the Insurance Corporation of British Columbia, the investigators stated that:

> Those observed as not wearing a restraint were asked about frequency of usage and reasons for not wearing a restraint at that time. Fifty-seven percent (57%) claimed they wore a restraint more than half the time, 14 percent about half the time, eight percent less than half the time, and 18 percent hardly ever or never. The main reasons for not wearing were:

| | |
|---|---|
| Short trip | 45% |
| Forgot/in a hurry | 20% |
| Belt uncomfortable/nuisance | 5% |
| In town/only wear on highway | 8% |
| I was wearing it (denial) | 6% |
| Belt does not work | 2% |
| Medical certificate | < 1% |
| Other | 13% |

When drivers in this safety belt survey were asked about the length of their current trip, it was found that a significantly greater percentage of non-wearers were engaged in short trips ($< 2$ km) than was the case for wearers (58.4% vs. 38.6%, respectively). By comparison, a significantly greater percent of wearers (17.4%) than non-wearers (8.1%) were on trips longer than 10 km.

Rationalized responses to people's views on risk of crash and distance of the trip have been made with regularity. For example, O'Day and Filkins wrote in the *UMTRI Research Review*:

> Statistics show that you are most likely to be in an accident when driving or riding at slow speeds and close to home. Researchers have found that more than 80 percent of all accidents occur at speeds of less than 40 miles an hour and that three out of four accidents causing death occur within 25 miles of home (1983, p. 5).

As is common in statistical analyses, the descriptors used—although important to people's views—were not directly relevant to their behavioral patterns. To illustrate, the researchers specified that three out of four accidents causing death occurred within 40 km (25 miles) of home. This could designate distances ranging from several blocks to 40 km (25 miles). The difference between two blocks and 40 km (25 miles) was too broad a descriptor for the average person. Forty kilometres could, for some people, mean a long trip, or for others, a mere ride close to home. The interpretation of 40 km is greatly influenced by people's experiences, cultures and geography of residence.

To gain a more insightful perspective on distance of trip and risk of accident we selected a sample of 1,000 accident-involved drivers (500 who were belted and 500 who were unbelted). We established that over 68 percent of the persons lived within the community where their accidents occurred or else they lived in the immediately adjacent environs. Generally speaking, for these drivers this meant having an accident within 15 to 20 kilometres of home.

While the unbelted drivers were slightly overrepresented in this "close to home" group when compared to those wearing safety belts (69% vs. 68% of their respective totals), the difference was not significant. Based on the literature concerning safety belt non-use which clearly indicates a trend for non-use to be associated with short, local trips, the difference detailed above was somewhat smaller than might have been anticipated. It is worth noting, however, that very short trips (e.g., a few blocks or within local residential areas) were impossible to isolate with the accuracy of the locational information available. Thus any differences between belted and unbelted driver representation on brief excursions would have been considerably diluted.

# Highways and City Streets

Most of the problems of daily life may be mastered by following a pattern or routine. There is no need to define or redefine situations which have occurred so many times. Definition is related to approved ways of thinking by groups. One in-group process of thinking suggests that mishaps resulting in serious injury are considerably more likely to happen on highways than on city streets. Velocity is at the root of reasoning. As one driver put it:

> If you're doing a hundred or more and you hit somebody or go
> off the road, it's gotta be a serious accident.

The quote exemplifies a common rationality for non-use of safety belts in the city, particularly in residential areas. A reason for stressing use on highways was turned around into a reason for justifying non-use in urban and suburban areas.

Additional weight is accorded to the potential severity of highway crashes. Dramatic pile-ups of three, four or more cars are a common gauge for danger and risk. According to some drivers, multi-vehicle accidents occur most often on freeways or highways. One young man, who considers himself to be, overall, a safety belt wearer, illustrated:

> Quite often I don't wear them when I'm just driving around town,
> because it's pretty safe. Always on the freeway though. That's
> where you see the big pile-ups.

There was considerable debate on the character of roadways carrying different risks. While some people endorsed this notion as a matter of fact, others characterized it as "silly," asserting that accidents are as likely to happen in the city as on the highway. There was some consensus that the risk of mishap may not be as differentially distributed between residential street and highway as previously thought. However, severity of mishap definitely was greater for highways than city streets.

Empirical investigators have long been interested in the topic of the relative and absolute risks between highway and city street travel. Their interpretations differ a great deal from people's commonsense views. For example, Cooper (1985) reported that in British Columbia the risk of a driver having an injury-producing accident on city streets, when driving exposure is taken into account, is over twice as high as the risk of such a crash on a highway. An analysis of the 1986 British Columbia accident database showed that 82 percent of all traffic crashes occurred on city streets and arterials while only 13 percent were identified as highway-related. Five percent were not definable as either urban or highway and these included, among other things, off-road operations.

Furthermore, the big pile-ups alluded to by the previously quoted interviewee are not found to occur more often on highways. Eighty-one percent of accidents involving three or more vehicles in British Columbia during 1986 occurred on city streets and 14% on highways. These percentages were almost identical to those for overall accident involvement given above.

Interview data collected from drivers as part of the Corporation's province-wide roadside safety belt survey supported the contention that belt wearing is more common on highways than on city streets. When the researchers asked drivers to describe their current trip in terms of highway-involved driving, a greater percentage of restrained than unrestrained drivers (21.6% vs. 11.9% respectively) outlined that their trips involved some highway travel (significant at $p < .01$). Accident data confirmed the additional hazard associated with highway driving. The greater speeds on highways resulted in 2.8% of the accident-involved drivers being moderately-to-severely injured as opposed to only 0.8% of the drivers involved in accidents on city streets. The difference was significant at $p < .01$. Safety belt wearing for drivers in British Columbia was close to 80% at the time of the study.

The empirical descriptions of "what is" regarding city streets, highways, accident rates and safety belt usage accent some everyday assumptions, and debunk others. The risk of being seriously injured when in a collision is greater on highways than on city streets. But, the chance of being involved in an injury-producing crash on city streets is statistically greater than on highways.

# Traffic Density

Everyday accounts of danger on the roadway often included special emphasis on the density of traffic found on highways or city streets at any given time. Professed safety belt wearers and non-wearers alike generalized that normal drivers make decisions on the basis of traffic. For many people, a small amount of traffic relates to a small risk of mishap. Drivers may take more chances at this time, but because of low traffic density a crash is not likely to happen. From another perspective, drivers may judge their driving competence on the basis of how well they can negotiate rush hour traffic or overall high density traffic.

In a recent study on young drivers, we found that the majority of respondents who were involved in injury-producing crashes considered themselves to be cautious and competent (Rothe, 1987). Both of these driving qualities were closely referenced to density of traffic, in particular, heavy or rush-hour traffic. The young drivers (16 to 21 years old) believed that dense traffic situations demanded greater caution and driving competence. The major reason for the extra attention to driving was the unpredictability of other drivers. Young drivers felt uncomfortable and nervous because they had no control over other people's actions during rush-hour times.

On a more general level, the decision not to wear safety belts can reflect circumstances related to traffic density. The number of vehicles on streets prevailed in the interviews as a real focus for wearing safety belts. Some motorists apparently believe that it is proper and safe to drive without a safety belt during the small hours of the morning. There is little traffic so there is little chance of a crash and no real need for a safety belt. One young man exemplified this form of reasoning when he spoke about a weekend nighttime experience:

> It didn't really seem necessary (to wear a safety belt) because it was about three in the morning and there were hardly any cars on the road. There was no chance we would have an accident.

The interviewee's behavior is confirmed by empirical research. A specific example should prove valuable. In a 1982 study in British Columbia (Mercer, 1982), 7,380 drivers were stopped during four consecutive nights between 9:00 p.m. and 3:00 a.m. The proportion of drivers wearing safety belts by time period is illustrated in the following table:

| Time | Safety Belt Use (%) |
|------|---------------------|
| 9:00 – 10:30 a.m. | 61.3 |
| 10:30 – midnight | 58.2 |
| midnight – 1:30 a.m. | 55.0 |
| 1:30 – 3:00 a.m. | 49.9 |

As the night progresses, the extent of safety belt wearing decreases. The feeling of reduced risk experienced in the middle of the night when there is a lower traffic density may contribute to the lower safety belt wearing percentages illustrated above, although the increasing proportion of drinking drivers may also play a role.

Some drivers measure risk of mishap and traffic density according to street location in an urban setting. The belief is that not only are city streets safer than highways but some side streets are safer (and less likely to be policed) than other streets. It is not unusual, therefore, to find that drivers who have had a few drinks at a party use the side streets to get home. Furthermore, to not follow the "buckle-up" rule at night while driving on an unpretentious sidestreet is considered to be legitimate.

"I liked the way you kicked that tire. Very few of these young kids today understand the finer points of a quality vehicle."

# CHAPTER 4

# THE LAYPERSON AND TECHNOLOGY

# Introduction

As members of society we have a more or less coherent system of knowledge. Depending on our practical interests, we tend to be satisfied with our knowledge that certain means and procedures achieve certain desired or undesired results. The German philosopher Schutz wrote:

> We use the most complicated gadgets prepared by a very advanced technology without knowing how the contrivances work. No car driver is supposed to be familiar with the laws of mechanics, no radio listener with those of electronics. One may even be a successful businessman without an insight into the functioning of the market, or a banker without a smattering of monetary theory (1971).

The layperson uses procedures that may be trusted without clearly understanding them. Most of the procedures are linked to technology which, besides being a means to an end, is also a human activity.

Safety belts are simple technological devices implanted into large technological innovations called motor vehicles. A major goal for the development of safety belts is to reduce vehicle occupants' indifference toward their own safety. They are designed and installed so that drivers and passengers can no longer avoid direct responsibility for their health in the event of a crash. They can no longer blame chance as the rationalization for hitting their heads against windshields.

Unlike other technological innovations such as automatic transmissions, power brakes or power steering, the safety belt's rationale is prevention. On any normal trip, belts do not contribute to any tangible benefit. Most of us never see them work. Safety belt usefulness is not measured in terms of immediate driving consequences like a fuel-injected engine, which adds immediate power when a driver accelerates to pass another vehicle in a short space. Power steering adds to the comfort of driving. Cruise control helps the driver become involved in a more leisurely trip without the demand of acceleration and without the worry of exceeding the speed limit and thereby risking a citation.

Safety belts are worn "just in case." Much like smoke alarms in a house, safety belts are there without a great emphasis on their proper working condition or ultimate proof of need. While discussing this with a fire prevention officer, it was made clear that according to his surveys, up to 80 percent of homeowners do not check to see whether their smoke alarms work properly. About 50 percent of these homeowners are unaware that their devices may require new batteries every so often. McDonalds' restaurants recognize this volatile reality by setting aside several weeks a year when customers not only buy a "Big Mac" but they are also given literature on home smoke-alarm systems and the need to change batteries. For a little extra money, the Big Mac buyer can also purchase a battery. Similarly, for a little extra time and care, a car owner can make sure that the safety belts are operating properly.

# Maintaining Safety Belts

As lay people, we take the mechanical workings of safety belts for granted. This is not unusual since we do not have the time and inclination to become informed about all the technicalities and implications that are associated with items we use. Safety belts are ready-made tools which we use most often without unexpected proof of utility. The following analogy of a man-on-the-street and risk nicely portrays the safety belt issue:

> He will not cross the bridge before he reaches it, and he takes it for granted that he will find a bridge when he needs it and that it will be strong enough to carry him (Schutz, 1971, p. 130).

A common theme supported by motorists is that proper operation of safety belts—namely, safe and convenient usage—is not part of a frame of reference governed by relevant information. In lengthy discussions with drivers, a researcher wondered aloud about the number of people who drive with safety belts that either do not work or that are in some way defective. "Probably quite a few" was the collective response. "Who ever checks their safety belts?" quipped one member. "Who cares?" replied others. For the motorists, the condition of their safety belts, whether they operate or will operate properly in an emergency is at most a minimal concern or no concern at all. To get at the roots of organized behavior concerning technology, motorists were queried about the 12-point summer-vacation checkups offered by some service stations. Specifically, they were asked if the inspection included safety belts. Nobody was really sure. The most common guess was that safety belts were probably excluded. One participant personified others' thoughts by stating that if safety belt inspections did exist and if an inspection revealed a problem with the safety belts, most people would ignore it anyway and "just leave it." Others, too, felt that repairing a faulty restraint is low on the list of motorists' priorities. Most people would consider it as a waste of money.

To gather deep-rooted knowledge on motorists' sentiments, the researcher admitted that he too places restraints low on his list of repair priorities, even though he is a "believer" in safety belts. "You're as bad as us," was a collective response. The interviewer wondered aloud about this apparent inconsistency. How can someone be committed to safety belt use, yet relegate its maintenance and repair to the bottom of the priority list? Some participants excused the investigator by inferring that he was probably not alone in this contradiction. One discussant emphasized his point with the following story of a safety-conscious friend:

> He's the kind of guy that walks around his car before he gets in, checking the tires and things—who would probably never think of determining whether or not his safety belts would function properly in the event of a mishap. Like him, most people probably regard safety belts as ineffective or else don't think they'll get into an accident.

Wherever we went, safety belt maintenance or lack of it received prominent discussion. One participant told of driving for nearly two months without wearing safety belts. As the driver related, "The spring or something was broken on the driver's belt, making it impossible to fasten." In the meantime he ordered a new car. To establish the worth of his present automobile, the driver had received an estimate from a car dealer. From his point of view, fixing the inoperative safety belt would have been like "throwing money in the street" because the repair would not have enhanced the value of the vehicle. The driver was then asked if he would repair the belt if he decided to keep the car. "Probably not," the gentleman replied, "It's one of those things that you'd never get around to." Similar feelings were repeatedly expressed. It would be unlikely for drivers to take the trouble repairing inoperative belts. One discussant cited cost as a factor:

> You get charged 40 or 50 dollars an hour for car repairs. You want to spend that money on something worthwhile. It's not that I don't think that safety belts are worthwhile, it's just that . . . .

He did not finish his sentence. But clearly everyone knew what was meant. Restraints do not really count in our vehicle maintenance scheme.

Other rationales were provided. For example, it was reasoned that some mechanical things like brakes and steering, if left unrepaired, have a direct bearing on your safety. These items would be at the top of a motorist's repair list. Safety belts, however, are like dashboard clocks without which you can "get by." You may operate the car without noticing that they are in need of repair. Certain problems, if left unattended, can cause accidents but a broken safety belt does not.

Unrepaired safety belts are invisible. They are not manifested in our line of vision and mental scrutiny. To a certain degree, broken safety belts are lived-through by drivers and passengers. However, other technological features which are in unrepaired condition become more obvious. They are seen and noticed, even if not necessarily attended to. For example, several interviewees observed that they had driven their vehicles on "tires that had seen better days." Others said that they had seen "all kinds" of cars on the road with faulty shock absorbers. Apparently, many people misunderstand the role of shock absorbers. As mentioned in the opening paragraph of this chapter, lay people do not know about such things, or as one interviewee related: "Hardly anyone ever thinks about them," even though they are crucial to a vehicle's safety. To illustrate how uninformed some people are about the technical importance of shock absorbers, one motorist explained that although someone told him that his shocks were "shot," still he drove for months before replacing them. Somewhat sheepishly, he apologized for his naiveté explaining that he thought shock absorbers only affected a vehicle's "ride."

Faulty safety belts, apparently, fall somewhat below shock absorbers on the hierarchy of repairability. Witness the following quote:

> If you were told your brakes needed repairing, you'd probably tend to it right away. Shock absorbers—you'd probably wait until it was convenient or when you had the cash. With safety belts most people wouldn't bother.

Another motorist volunteered the information that in her car, neither one of the front-seat restraints works. Both are stuck. They are "too long" and they "dangle." She usually puts them on "anyway," tucking the end under her bottom to give the appearance of use in case she gets stopped by a police officer. Other participants considered this scheme to be legitimate and quite common. One person volunteered:

> I got in his car and the belt was about a mile long. He told me to tuck it in so it looks like it's on.

In this vein, someone mentioned once seeing a T-shirt with a safety belt printed across the front. "Would this fool the cops?" he asked with a smile.

It was common to hear everyday people describe their safety belts as being worn almost threadbare or as not retracting properly. Yet, when asked, few drivers would operate their cars with faulty steering or brakes. "You'd have to be crazy to do that," said one driver, "Driving with faulty safety belts is 'no problem.'" Apparently, incongruity is avoided by not regarding safety belts as part of the vehicle's safety equipment—or at least not really part of that equipment. A story was told of a friend who, some years ago, had his car rejected at a motor vehicle inspection station because the safety belts were inoperative. The speaker regarded this as grossly unfair, adding that he was put to some expense for "something that isn't all that important." There was general agreement with this assessment.

From a technical perspective, it appears that the most common cause of inoperative safety belts is twisted webbing in outboard rear-seat automatic locking retractors. Children and even adults often get the webbing twisted when releasing the belts and this causes the retractor to jam before the belt can fully return to the storage position. Since the retractor will not release the webbing for extraction until it has first been fully retracted, the restraint system is rendered inoperative. While the remedy usually only involves an hour or so of labor in opening-up and freeing the retractor, some garages or dealers may simply suggest replacing the entire belt system. This change can be quite expensive.

Broken retractor springs may also occur and this leaves the belt in the fully extended mode and makes adjustment impossible. Such a situation, and even a weakened spring which results in slow retraction, can result in further damage when loose webbing is caught in the door thereby weakening the fibres. Retractor efficiency is also compromised by the accumulation of dirt on the belt webbing.

The third most common cause of safety belt inoperation is the jamming of buckles by coins, hair pins, bottle caps and other small items. The only remedy for such a situation is the replacement of the entire restraint, including the retractor (where applicable). For a new front outboard restraint system the total cost may be several hundred dollars.

There are no reliable estimates of how many safety belts in currently-driven vehicles are inoperative since such cases are reported infrequently to authorities in Canada. Obviously, when motor vehicle operators are aware that their safety belt problems result from poor maintenance, they are unlikely to submit them for consideration as manufacturing defects, which is all the federal authorities are mandated to investigate.

Not only do safety belts tend to be removed from the people's general frames of reference regarding mechanical maintenance, they can also be neglected when it comes to cleaning cars. Although we spend a great deal of time scrubbing and waxing the body, vacuuming the interior, washing the windows and dusting the dashboard, we are not likely to check and clean the safety belts. They are in the spools, hanging on the side, forgotten.

Yet, clean-up of safety belts is an important part of preparatory thinking. Nobody likes to wear a dirty safety belt over clean formal wear. The decision, therefore, not to buckle up because the belt is dirty is a decision likely to be made by both self-defined wearers and non-wearers alike. One lady told us that she never puts on safety belts if she's wearing a white or light-colored blouse or dress. The reason, she said, is that her belts are "old and dirty" and are likely to leave a mark on her clothing. Although she tried cleaning them once, they "stayed damp for ages." To add insult to injury, they remained just as dirty after the wash. When the researcher suggested that perhaps the belt should be replaced, she, with the vocal support of other motorists, found the idea laughable. "It would be a waste of money," she added. She justified her occasional non-use by noting that she just drives around town "anyway." In general, participants felt that the lady's very small risk of an accident was worth it, as she was certain to soil her clothing if she buckled up. If she were ever involved in an accident and told the police that the reason she was unbuckled was because the safety belt was dirty, she would feel foolish. "But," she added, "I'm not going to have an accident just driving a few miles."

The body of accounts offered by drivers contained numerous instances of non-use based on the observation that the safety belt was so soiled or wet that it would ruin one's clothing if worn. Consider:

> One week ago my friend didn't realize that the passenger's safety belt had fresh mud on it. I wasn't about to put a dirty safety belt on after it had been dragged across the city.

> The safety belt had been stuck in the door so part of it had been rained upon. I refused to wear a wet and dirty belt so I drove without it on.

Even if dry and clean, the safety belt may produce undesirable consequences:

> I didn't put it on because I was wearing a very nice outfit that would wrinkle if I had to strap myself in.

> I did not wear my safety belt because the shoulder strap is particularly tight, and I didn't want to wrinkle the silk blouse I had spent an hour ironing.

Drivers' perspectives clearly illustrate a common gap between a technological innovation for prevention and thought patterns needed to maintain the innovation at high levels of efficiency. The state of safety belt preparedness in anticipation of potential need does not parallel the preparedness of, for example, proper brakes, steering wheels or transmissions.

# How Can They Work

A broad theme commonly discerned as "real" was that few people knew how safety belts are supposed to work.

Although at first sight this may be considered intrinsically irrelevant, a closer look at the matter may prove otherwise. As we previously stated, people do not have to know the inner workings of all technological devices. As long as they do what they are supposed to do we are satisfied. Safety belts, however, are a little different. Most of us will never know what safety belts will do in an accident. Unless we are shown, our imaginations are the only sources of inspiration. The converse of the knowing thesis now becomes highly relevant. If we do not know how safety belts work, how will we know if they are not going to work? To examine the question at face value, we asked groups of motorists to provide us with the public knowledge concerning this question.

One driver answered that she has experimented with her restraint system. With her belt in place, she leaned forward simulating a collision. To her dismay her head still hit the steering wheel. "How can this be any good?" she queried her colleagues. A lady responded to the challenge. She explained that the force of an impact would automatically tighten the safety belt, thereby preventing forward motion. However she footnoted her claim by stating she was not certain. She believed that her restraints also did not work properly. Like the previous speaker she had, in fact, leaned forward quickly and dramatically and detected no appreciable difference in "tightness." Other respondents shrugged their shoulders, symbolizing a consensus lack of knowledge. This became recognizable when a third speaker noted that both of the ladies' safety belts are probably not working properly. Others eagerly nodded in agreement.

A driver from central British Columbia said that many people probably do not wear "modern" safety belts because they fit so loosely as to give you the feeling that they're not really doing anything. People do not trust the potential based on their observations of the real. Although the participant believed that safety belts come into action upon impact, he wondered aloud how many people think they're "just there." From his point of view, if the chest strap were "tighter" people might have more faith in the ultimate benefit. They might then be more inclined to wear them.

Based on the preceding discussion patterns, it is obvious that the technical operation of safety belts appears too sophisticated for the commonsense understanding of the layperson. Many people do not know that in the most common form of occupant restraint currently in use (the "three-point" manual lap-shoulder belt), a form of locking retractor mechanism is employed to store the webbing. The most prevalent retractor types are the automatic locking retractor (ALR) and the emergency locking retractor (ELR).

The automatic locking retractor is designed to allow the occupant to have full belt extension fit. Once it is sufficiently extended using a consistent extraction motion, it locks into place. The emergency locking retractor mechanism, on the other hand, is maintained snugly around the person. It allows unrestricted normal movement but is activated by sudden deceleration or webbing movement. Some new car models have incorporated webbing pre-tensioning devices which are designed to reduce spool-out and belt slack during the initial stages of an impact.

Because the ELR belt allows unrestricted movement of the occupant during normal operation of a vehicle, some people lack confidence in the belt's design to effectively lock and restrain them during a crash. Drivers and passengers must have faith that the emergency locking retractor will, in fact, lock upon impact. Such faith in technology is not readily accepted by some people.

# The Case for Back Seats

The back seat of a vehicle may be considered an area that fosters secondary involvement. The preferential seating is the front seat. This is where the driver is located and social control of in-car events occurs.

Passengers in back seats tend to feel obliged to sustain at least a minimal involvement in social discourse. To do so they attempt to interact with front-seat passengers without major discomfort. Safety belts may impinge on their natural body movements whenever conversation with front-seat occupants ensues. To compensate for the cumbersomeness, safety belts are not worn, or they are undone. It is considered proper not to wear rear safety belts so that conversations may happen more easily with front-seat occupants. Many safety belt wearers and non-wearers also believe that not to wear safety belts in the back carries no great risk.

In group discussions and biographical sketches, we learned firsthand why motorists considered back seats safer than front seats. Risk of injury in back seats was reduced because they contain fewer objects that can harm occupants in a collision. There are no windshields, steering wheels or dashboards. In the various interview sessions conducted, we found that participants had heard or read that rear safety belt use is actually dangerous, should one have a serious accident.

To precipitate discussion on the issue, the group leader asked respondents why people, whose cars have no restraint system, generally installed only front-seat restraints. "Probably because the back seat is pretty safe as it is," was a representative reply. While it was believed that you could, in a major crash, get injured in the back, your chances of incurring serious injury were much lower in the rear than in the front:

"In a head-on collision you'd just bounce off the front seats," said one citizen. Another noted that the back seat of late-model cars is safe, because the cars are often very small and they have no windows. "Not like in the older cars where there was lots of glass." Someone mentioned the almost cocoon-like back seats of some cars: "You've got nowhere to go, not like the front where you go through the window." One participant said that it would be a waste of time for anybody to install rear safety belts because "they just get tangled up anyway." "I haven't seen mine for years," he emphasized. Another participant agreed and noted that he only "dug out" the back safety belts when he put his car up for sale.

One lady, describing her views on rear safety belts, argued that they were useless because, for the most part, they are only of the "lap" variety. "They won't prevent whiplash," she noted, adding that this is the most common injury incurred in automobile accidents. Someone else said that "expensive" cars have shoulder restraints in the back, though he couldn't be specific as to which ones. Another participant said that he had "heard" that rear shoulder restraints were going to be "phased in" as standard equipment on all cars, much like the high-mount rear brakelight. It was remarked that for the most part it is not really necessary for back-seat passengers to buckle up "anyway" because the back seat is relatively safe when compared to the front.

One firmly held principle was that the rear seat was safer than the front seat. It was a matter of fact. From drivers' points of view, back seats are ambiguous with respect to the need for safety devices like safety belts. It seems that people believe that there is a kind of invisible physical membrane which helps maintain a safe driving environment.

The belief in such a level of security for the back seat is challenged by traffic safety professionals. While researchers such as Evans and Frick (1987) have confirmed a moderate fatality-risk advantage for unbelted occupants in rear seating positions over those in the front, the back seat is by no means the "safe haven" for unrestrained passengers that our interviewees believed. During 1986 in British Columbia, a slightly greater proportion of unbelted back-seat occupants than front-seat occupants were taken, although not necessarily admitted, to hospital (29.3% vs. 26.5%). In terms of police-assessed injury, these front-seat occupants were more likely to suffer damage in excess of bruises than were the back-seat occupants (14.2% vs. 12.2%). While such evidence is somewhat inconsistent, nevertheless it reinforces the impression that if unbelted occupants are indeed safer in the back seats of automobiles it is not by a wide margin.

# Attenuating or Accentuating Injuries

It was not unusual to discover that many drivers have only a minimal understanding, or a faulty understanding, of safety belts' role and potential. "What do safety belts do?" motorists were asked. Some responses were, "keeping you from getting thrown from the car," "keeping you from going through the windshield," and "keeping you from hitting the dashboard." Jokingly, one added, "Keeping you from getting a fine." This driver "really doubts" that safety belts would effectively protect passengers in an accident of any magnitude, adding that they would be "useless" if you were broadsided. "They won't keep your head off the side window," he noted. Apparently, his wife was in such an accident and though she was buckled up she still was injured. "It wouldn't have mattered how many safety belts she was wearing," he said. A university student told a story about a woman suffering a miscarriage after a minor accident. "If she wasn't wearing a safety belt, it wouldn't have happened," he said.

Such a discrepancy between the date of availability (manufacture) of safety belts and people's arrival at a definition of benefit and usage may be defined as culture lag. It is not simply the case that the inventor invents it and the public merely accepts it en masse and immediately. Rather, it takes time for an item of technology such as safety belts to be absorbed, diffused or considered legitimate by participants in a particular culture. And there is no guarantee that complete absorption, diffusion or perceived legitimacy will be achieved. Some innovations never penetrate the public consciousness in the lifetime of their inventors or advocates. Although technicians and specialists in the discipline are quick to recognize the benefits of a particular technological innovation, members of the non-technical, non-specialized public at large do so less quickly, if at all. They cannot be chastised for this. They have their established ways, and sometimes these are contrary to the ways of the experts.

Although research has established that the proper wearing of safety belts attenuates the likelihood and seriousness of injury, some motorists are quick to refute it. Based on their experience, safety belts may actually accentuate the severity of injury.

There are "all kinds" of accidents wherein safety belts are considered totally ineffective at preventing or minimizing injury. It was not unusual for motorists to maintain that safety belt effectiveness was restricted to injuries that result from dramatic forward motion—motion that happens in head-on collisions. We heard numerous accounts where discussants considered safety belts to be useless in preventing injuries that might result from dramatic lateral motion—such as "when you're broadsided or wrap your car around a telephone pole."

An extended conversation segment to further illustrate the accentuation principle, centred around one particular speaker who noted that:

> Safety belts only "really" help in a frontal collision. There must be a lot of these because "used front-end parts are hard to get from the wrecker." He said that safety belts are useless in a broadside collision. A side window can do a lot of damage to one's head. As proof he told of witnessing such an accident last year. He was first to arrive on the scene after a severe collision between two vehicles. Both drivers appeared to have broken necks and head injuries, which he attributed to smashing into the side windows and "bouncing back." Later, he heard on the radio that one of the drivers died. Both were wearing safety belts, he noted. He then added that "nothing could've saved them."

The suspicion with which some safety belt non-wearers view empirical research on risk and the commonsense versions of risk which they share provides, for them, occasional reinforcement. It is not unusual to leaf through a newspaper and find a report on a serious automobile crash where the driver's life was "saved" because he was not wearing a safety belt. Recently, the following article appeared in *The Vancouver Sun*:

### Vancouver Survivor Didn't Use Seatbelt, Inquest Told

> One of three survivors of a fatal highway collision February 6 was thrown free of the wreck after apparently leaving his seatbelt undone, a coroner's inquest was told Wednesday. The two youths beside him and two others behind him were crushed when a tractor-trailer collided with their van. All four buckled up, although one other safety belt broke from the force of the impact. However, a Transport Canada safety expert insisted the surviving youth would have suffered fewer injuries if he'd been buckled up (Morton, 1987).

Conversations with police constables often lead to descriptions of their experience where they were called to crashes only to discover that the unbelted drivers were thrown to safety. These experiences provide individual members of the police with a lore of understanding. So they operate a police cruiser without buckling up. We established that other drivers witness this and therefore question the need to wear them. One lady indicated that her brother is an RCMP officer. He never uses safety belts. "He has seen too much." Among other things such as the inconvenience of a safety belt during a time of crisis, the officer does not endorse the preventative potential of safety belts. Under the circumstances, safety belt non-wearers' impressions of reality concerning risk and safety belt non-wearing is regularly sustained and even subsidized by other institutional representatives.

Motorists never hesitated to document their viewpoint with stories about friends who were involved in accidents of the sort wherein "safety belts don't do any good." Observe the following discussion:

> One motorist stated that the only time he wears safety belts is when he "has a feeling" there will be a police check or he actually sees a roadblock. "Many times I've driven with my knees while I get the damned thing on," he noted. When asked why he routinely did not use belts, he replied that it was "sort of a personal thing," and added that there are good reasons to not wear them. He recounted a story of a woman being burned alive because her safety belt prevented her from escaping from her overturned vehicle. He told another story about a man who suffered severe internal damage in a minor mishap: "The safety belt crushed his guts." The interviewer said that he would be interested in learning more about such incidents and asked the participant if he could provide some references. Beyond mention of having "heard about them from somebody," he was unable to. The interviewer asked him to consider the possibility that such stories may be mere "urban tales," like the fifty-dollar Porsche, the cat in the microwave oven, or the cement-filled Cadillac. No, he insisted, the material he'd heard about serious injury resulting from safety belt use was indisputably true.

Like the example just cited, many drivers had similar tales of woe about how safety belts contributed to injury. However, most participants had merely "heard" about the pathogenic potential of safety belts. They were unable to specify the source of their presentations. Nevertheless, they regarded such information as factual. Whenever they were requested to provide verbal documentation on such highly visible events, the respondents became defensive. Some became hostile and emotional. They felt that their integrity was being questioned. Although they did not substantiate their stories, still they felt that the tales were factual because of assumed personal reference.

One of the few accounts of personal experience provided some dramatic images. A gentleman explained that during his driving life he has been involved in numerous mishaps, of which two were very serious. One accident resulted in a six-month stay in the hospital, numerous joint pins, and other medical fixes. According to the fellow's girlfriend, "He broke nearly every bone in his body." From the driver's point of view, the only reason he is still alive today is because he was not wearing his safety belt. In one accident he was thrown clear from his car before it rolled, which was flattened to the doorline, and then exploded. The crash sounded like a Hollywood stunt. "It probably looked like one, too," said the participant. According to the interviewee, medical personnel at the site of the crash told him that he "would have blown up with the car" if he had been buckled up.

In his second accident he was "T-boned" or broadsided by a dump truck. At the moment of impact, the motorist said that he was thrown to the other side of the seat (apparently contrary to the accepted laws of motion) "as the window exploded." Again he reiterated his belief that he "wouldn't be here to tell the story" had he been wearing safety belts. Consequently, the speaker never wears safety belts, though he has been cited for non-use "three or four" times by the police. He will buckle up when he spots the police but he refuses to do so otherwise. He is committed to the notion that people are better off not wearing safety belts if they are involved in a serious accident. For other kinds of crashes, especially the non-serious ones, it does not really matter whether a safety belt is worn or not.

Some participants documented their points of view with "sureness." Frequently, they made reference to the "unsound" nature of safety belt research and the political character of mandatory-use legislation. The researcher suggested that there was ample evidence documenting the injury-reduction capabilities of safety belts, and that it was unfair to classify the basis of the legislation as "speculation." A group participant replied that if the "effectiveness of safety belt use was truly documented, wouldn't it be the case that use would be mandatory everywhere and not just in a few jurisdictions? Would it not be a federal matter? Does the government of, say, Alberta, know something that British Columbia's does not?" (Alberta has since implemented mandatory safety belt legislation.)

The driver suggested that the safety belt issue was political, and that the legislation had nothing to do with the alleged assets or liabilities of restraints. He said that there is "evidence" that in some cases safety belts "make injuries worse."

There was some discussion regarding why back seat belt use is still legally required, even though it has been "shown" to be potentially dangerous. Will the government consider repealing some aspects of the legislation in the interest of safety and the prevention of snapped spines? Not likely, a discussant replied to his colleague. From his point of view, the original legislation making safety belt use mandatory was not based on "solid" research.

Further rationalization of the accentuation principle included the two-kinds-of-accidents theory. The first kind of crashes is so serious that nothing is going to save the occupant from injury. The second kind is so benign that it does not matter whether the occupant is wearing a safety belt. Therefore, according to one driver, wearing safety belts is a "total waste of time," save for the fact that in British Columbia you might get a fine if caught driving unrestrained. Opposition to the theory was based on the oversimplification of a "black and white" scenario. There is the possibility of a "middle range" accident which is somewhere between the benign and the fatal. Within this circumstance safety belt wearing would be effective in preventing or minimizing injury. Although supporters of the "black and white" theory eventually softened their stance, still they maintained a benchmark position. They admitted the existence of more-than-benign, less-than-fatal mishaps but they emphasized that "most" crashes are benign. They thereby concluded that wearing belts is a "total waste of time."

After careful reading of all our interview data sources we detected a certain fatalism: Uniformly and clearly, citizens were of the opinion that for some mishaps, little, short of prayer, would save the victims from injury or death—and safety belts definitely would not. A saving grace to this internalized view is the follow-up notion that such accidents are few and far between, and of a frequency so limited that hardly anyone would experience one in the course of a lifetime. In all of the province-wide discussion groups, few members—even after a long accumulation of driving hours—experienced major crashes causing serious injury or death.

For better or worse, our driving experiences are largely experiences of routines. Part of the routines may be our dependence on "luck." For some drivers, "luck" is considered to be a noteworthy and tangible element when they establish the attenuating chance of injury. A popular line of reasoning is that people who survive serious crashes do so not for reasons of proper belt use but more for reasons of luck. The relationship between survival and safety belts is defined as apparent, but not as real. One driver stated his belief clearly by explaining that it would be just as reasonable to say that a driver lived through a serious accident because a St. Christopher's medal was being worn or a plastic Jesus figure was on the dashboard. Accordingly, nobody can be really sure, ever, why a person survives a crash. Whenever motorists were told that there was a considerable body of scientific literature claiming the injury-reducing potential of safety belts, some participants repeated "scientific" in a tone of voice that suggested they had placed quotation marks around it. "Nothing has really been proven beyond doubt," one driver noted. He reemphasized the commonsense assumption shared by many drivers that luck is the key element in surviving a major crash. Indeed there was general agreement that luck played a major role in staying alive, whether we survive a serious auto mishap or "beat" cancer. A conclusion drawn by a motorist was that for most types of accidents safety belts are not necessary and they offer absolutely no protection. Support for this point of view was overwhelming.

> A safety belt won't save you from whiplash. This is the common injury in urban-area mishaps. Nor will safety belts prevent you from sustaining injuries in a broadside collision. And in a really bad accident, nothing will save you but blind luck.

The application of luck as a device to explain life events is common. People are considered lucky if they miss an accident regardless of driving competence, get a job regardless of qualifications, have a bright child, or make a productive decision. Escaping injury is just another event achieved through luck. It orients individuals away from responsibility toward an unexplainable deterministic side of life.

# Retrofitting or Adding To

When we speak of people's attitudes about the legitimacy of safety belt non-wearing behavior, we find it useful to discuss surrogate issues which contribute to the clarification of the matter. One such issue is refitting a car that has no safety belts.

A theme considered worthy of exploring further was that vintage cars should not be required to have safety belts. To highlight the concern, we include the following contentious exchange:

> A participant elaborated that he owns a vintage-designated 1953 Chevrolet that he had restored to near concours d'elegance condition. It is a point of pride for him that everything on the vehicle is as close to the original as it could possibly be. Safety belts would seriously flaw this goal: "Safety belts were neither standard issue nor in common use in 1953," explained the car buff. Vintage cars are his hobby, and he is heavily involved in the hobbyist subculture. To his knowledge, no one he knows who owns a restored automobile would even consider adding safety belts. The aesthetics of such an addition would be offensive to purist sensibilities. "Besides," he noted, "these cars only get driven on special occasions and their owners 'baby' them as much on the road as they do off." By this he meant that vintage car owners can be counted on to operate their vehicles with extreme caution.

"When you've put that much work and money into something, you're not going to drive like a maniac," he said. The interviewer raised the question of other vehicles on the road and pointed out the possibility of mishaps that occur independent of the skill, caution, and concern of one driver. Being rear-ended while stopped in traffic was cited as an example of such a mishap, and the injury-reducing potential of restraint use was mentioned. "Yes," he agreed, "uncontrollable accidents are a possibility but a slim one." "There is a risk," he noted, "but it is one worth taking to keep your vehicle original."

Another focus of retrofitting is economics. It is a fact that older cars have no safety belts. It is a general belief that poor people buy old cars. They do so because of their poor economic standing. If they have little money they cannot afford to spend the money needed for retrofits. The persons who buy older cars are probably "financially strapped" and are not able to bear the additional expense.

What about a government-ordered retrofit on all cars, both older and vintage, currently exempt from safety belts? Would this work? None of the motorists we met endorsed such an order. It would penalize certain groups in society, they noted, again because most older cars are driven by the poor and the young. An alternate scenario was then presented to drivers. For many, and particularly the young, older vehicles are as much a matter of choice as economics amongst some segments of the population. High-displacement, pre-pollution-control, pre-fuel-crisis vehicles are highly valued because of their performance characteristics. There was some agreement in principle. But the bottom line was that economic discrimination was sure to arise from government-mandated retrofit of all vehicles.

# Installing Child Seats

British Columbia, most Canadian provinces, and some American states have passed laws for mandatory child restraint usage. The "baby bucket" or "love bucket" requires little time and effort to place within the design of a vehicle's occupant restraint system. However, the placement of a child seat demands more thought and skill.

To get maximum safety effect from a child seat, it must be tethered. This means an anchor point must be located in the vehicle; a hole is drilled and an eye bolt is bolted on. The seat is then clamped to the eye bolt. The process requires initiative and a minimal knowledge of mechanics and tools. Also, the onus for installation is on the driver or vehicle owner. Many service station mechanics do not service or install child seats because they wish to stay away from possible liability cases in the event of a crash.

In 1983, the Insurance Corporation of British Columbia initiated a roadside survey to establish the extent to which preschoolers were placed in proper restraint systems, and to determine if the systems were properly installed. This survey pre-dated applicable legislation in the province, which was introduced in January, 1985. Figure 1 illustrates a quick overview of the relevant findings.

**Figure 1**
**Usage of Child Safety Seats Among Preschoolers**

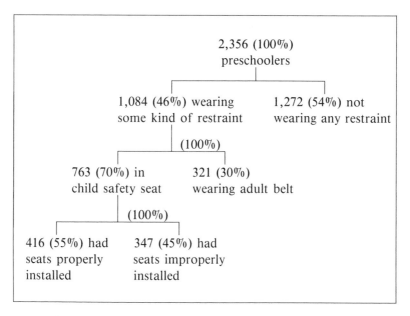

A review of the figures shows that although 70 percent of the children were placed in a safety seat, over 45 percent of these (347 out of 763) were improperly installed. Most often the tether strap was not anchored. The child seat was held only by a rear-seat lap belt. Yet, according to the Canadian Ministry of Transport, for maximum effectiveness the child seat must be tethered.

In a province-wide roadside survey undertaken by the Insurance Corporation of British Columbia in October, 1987, 15,123 vehicles were stopped. Of these, 1,145 occupants were under the age of five years. According to the research team:

While restraint usage is high among infants and young children (over 85 percent), it must be noted that a significant proportion of these individuals are using inappropriate forms of restraint (e.g., seven percent of those less than three years old and 44 percent of those three to five years old are wearing lap belts only). Parents may unwittingly be placing their children in quite unsafe conditions without understanding the implications of their behavior.

A further question in this survey asked the driver whether the back of their child seat was attached to the car with a separate strap (tether strap). The question was asked when a child or convertible seat was in the car, regardless of whether it was occupied. Only 44 percent responded that the seat was tethered, with the percentage being 46 percent if the seat was actually occupied. Guidelines suggest that all child and convertible seats should be tethered. This is an obvious point about which parents should be educated (B.C. Research, 1987, p. 24).

As evidenced in the surveys, within a span of four years from the original survey in 1983, adults have not yet reached the point at which they adopt the technology of child restraints properly according to design. This is in spite of recent provincial government legislation that child seats are mandatory and official guidelines specifying that all child and convertible seats must be properly tethered.

# About Other Vehicle Safety Technology

The safety-socialized person is pivotal in traffic safety. If drivers consider safety belts as second-rate gadgetry compared to other vehicle technology, it would be interesting to see how they feel about surrogate safety equipment such as high-mounted brakelights and motorcycle helmets. The attitudes toward the practical use of these innovations for non-tangible ends are as conspicuous as those for safety belt wearing.

Drivers were observed and questioned about safety practices during a province-wide safety belt survey. A significantly higher proportion of those wearing safety belts than of those not restrained reported using headlights in the daytime (74.0% vs. 63.3%). However, there were no measurable differences between the two groups in the relative frequencies reported of different circumstances under which daytime headlights would be used. In terms of brakelights, 8.3% of belted drivers in non factory-equipped vehicles had installed the new centre, high-mounted devices while only 4.4% of unbelted drivers in such vehicles had done so. Again, the difference was highly significant.

Overall, safety technology, unless directly proven effective, does not have the commitment of use as does technology concerning other areas of life. It is too difficult to observe safety belts in action. Consequently there is little **real** faith in the need to wear them. Unless more concerted efforts are made to illustrate physically how, when and why they work, profound shifts in attitudes are unlikely. This should not be typified as ignorance or naiveté. It is but one more example of how people relate to certain technology within their priorities of life.

This lack of faith in technology was clearly exhibited by respondents in our in-depth observational survey. Only 38% of those drivers interviewed were in favor of high-mounted brakelights. Most had no confidence in their utility (safety potential) and some even felt they were hazardous. Similarly, most drivers (78%) said they did not always use headlights during the daytime. A substantial proportion of these referred to the possibility of dead batteries as a tangible representation of their lack of faith in the utility of the concept. As with the province-wide survey results, a significantly higher proportion of safety belt wearers than non-wearers were observed with their headlights on.

Automobile-related technology is like any other technology for mass consumption. For it to be used, people need to see how it can benefit them in practical terms. This is especially true for safety technology. The time may never come for people to witness actual effectiveness. Therefore people's conceptions of safety devices are tainted by the ever-popular slogans, "Show me," or "Prove it." Because safety belts fall within this structure, people's suspicions of their effectiveness, hesitancy to maintain them properly, and susceptibility to drawing conclusions from anecdotal accounts should be expected.

# CHAPTER 5

# OTHER ACTIVITIES IN A CAR ARE MORE IMPORTANT THAN SAFETY BELTS

In chapter 4, we noted the use of the rear seat and its relationship to people's views of risk. In this chapter, we will expand on the use of the automobile other than just for transportation. The character of the automobile is such that it cannot be defined solely as a technological device used for transporting people from a point of origin to a destination. The car is a micro social setting, albeit a moving one, in which social meaning is shared and displayed. Dynamic interaction amongst vehicle occupants is so common and expected, that to deviate from this would be a cultural inconsistency. A vehicle may serve as a picnic site, smoking room, drinking lounge, lovers' bedroom, music chamber, or a combination of these at any given time.

In cars, parents discipline their children or nurse newborns. For children, the automobile is an enclosed moving playground where toys are available for long trips. Some businesses are specifically designed to operate on the premise that the automobile is a social environment. The drive-in theatre was synonymous with kissing and "making-out," drive-in restaurants cater to in-car food consumption, and drive-in banks contribute to in-car business transactions.

Despite the occurrence of in-car socialization activities while the vehicle is moving, occupants are—in many jurisdictions—mandated by law or in some areas requested by reason, to fasten their safety belts. The question which arises is how does safety belt wearing relate to the social organization within a vehicle?

In the descriptions that follow, it becomes clear that social activities in cars may necessitate that occupants not wear safety belts. It is simply more important to be, or be seen to be, involved in social activities than it is to abide by a strict safety code—that is, wearing safety belts at all times.

A general rule followed by many motorists is that if safety belts interfere with other in-car activities they are not worn at the outset, or they are unbuckled. Carrying on conversations in motor vehicles figure prominently within the rule. For example, motorists frequently claimed that buckling-up would effectively exclude back-seat passengers from conversation with those in the front. The following quote highlights the back-seat theme:

> I never wear one if I'm in the back seat. With the high seats in the front and the tapedeck on, you have to lean forward to get in on the conversation.

As well, many people with whom we spoke mentioned that eating, sleeping, and just assuming a comfortable position were made difficult by safety belt use. From time to time, these projects take priority over matters of safe practice. Consider the following examples:

> I bought an ice cream at the Dairy Queen and I couldn't really
> balance it anywhere while I put the belt on, so I thought I would
> wait until I finished to put it on. I didn't put it on because I was
> almost home by then.

> An occasion when I didn't wear my safety belt was when I was
> going on a long vacation by car to northern British Columbia. I
> didn't wear it because I was really tired and wanted to sleep. I was
> riding in the back seat so I thought it would be all right. I can't
> sleep while sitting up, and it's impossible to get comfortable while
> wearing a safety belt.

> The reason why I did not wear a safety belt was because the trip
> was so long and it was like a restriction. We were all sitting in the
> car for so long and were tired of sitting. The restraint of the safety
> belt was no help so I took it off so I could move freely in the car.

It was not unusual to hear people speak about unfastening their belts
to turn around and "discipline" children in the back seat. According
to one mother, her husband appreciates it when she controls the
children. He does the same thing when she's driving. Her children
frequently fight and argue, particularly on longer trips. "It drives us
nuts," she said. Other participants said that they, too, have had to
remove their belts to tend to children in the back seat. In the case of
one lady, it was not necessarily for discipline but to do such things as
wipe noses and mop up spilled drinks. Like her colleague, her
recollection was based on longer trips.

The mention of longer trips provoked other memories such as getting
a thermos or sandwiches and snacks from the back seat. This and other
back-seat retrievals require removal of the safety belt. It was considered
unreasonable to pull over to the side of the road and stop to perform
these operations. "My husband would think I was crazy if I said, 'okay,
stop the car, I've got to wipe Jenny's nose.' " Others agreed that
most—if not all—drivers would find such a request strange. "Nobody
would ever do that," one driver concluded with conviction. Other
motorists were in strong agreement.

Not one person with whom we spoke had any difficulty recalling
occasions where he or she did not use safety belts because of preference
for social activities. Impressions were left that every informant could
recall many related instances. Infant care stood out as a legitimate
reason for unfastening one's safety belt. The following abbreviated
narrative displays this theme:

> One young mother noted that she "often" tends to her baby—
> secure in an infant seat in the back—while her husband is driving.
> This operation, of course, entails the removal of her safety belt.
> "What could I do?" she said. "If the baby starts crying, it drives
> my husband crazy. I have to quieten her down."

The ongoing stream of events occurring in a car provided the basis of decisions as things happened. For example, one participant told of hearing on the car radio that soft drinks were on sale at a convenience store. She asked her son to check in the back of the station wagon to see if there were any bottles or cans they might return for deposit should they pass a store and decide to buy some soft drinks. Her son removed his safety belt and as they drove along, he peered over the seat into the cargo area. Others had seen or done similar things while driving. Spontaneous circumstances overruled decisions and habitual behavior about safety.

So often, reasons for not wearing a safety belt when a person was involved in social business while driving were accompanied by the disclaimer: "What could I do?" Drivers and passengers implicitly demonstrated that social acts had greater priority than safe driving actions. Consequently, there was nothing else they felt they could do within the awkward circumstances in which they found themselves. It was more expedient to break a safety law than to break a social rule or norm. As Bierstedt wrote:

> A norm, then, is a rule or a standard that governs our conduct in the social situations in which we participate. It is a societal expectation. It is a standard to which we are expected to conform whether we actually do so or not. It is a cultural specification that guides our conduct in society. It is a way of doing things, the way that is set for us by our society (1957, p. 217).

The automobile as a social microcosm reflects certain behaviors which are pervasive and prevail over other things such as, perhaps, safety. As a folk vehicle, the automobile exists to accommodate behavioral patterns surrounding such things as child-rearing, eating and drinking, tactfully interacting with others, and personal comfort. Attention to such in-car matters is considered appropriate and often predominant.

The risk that socializing has for causing accidents was noted by Rothe (1987). In analyzing interviews with 130 young drivers who were involved in injury-producing crashes, he found that fifteen of them admitted their driving performance was perhaps seriously influenced by loud music, and that four other drivers definitely linked talking with passengers to their crashes. Other activities that distracted drivers and contributed to crashes were: looking for specific addresses; seeing acquaintances on the sidewalk; looking for items in the car; eating, drinking or smoking; and cleaning the windows.

Rothe provided the following young-driver response to illustrate the real impact that socializing had just before a major accident:

Interviewer: Do you think that listening to the radio or just talking to your friends could have led to the accident?

Respondent: Yes . . . because you're listening to them and it's . . . you sort of . . . you test them . . . so, when they say . . . when . . . you're sort of talking to them and you're looking both ways and they go . . . O.K. go . . . usually you kind of . . . you know you look . . . but in this case, the person said oh, you can go . . . and I thought, yeah, I can go, but . . . I think otherwise maybe I would've waited but I'm not sure, but I think I would've if no one had said anything and so, if I didn't have anyone there to talk to, I don't know . . . maybe I would've thought a bit (1987, p. 64).

Engaging in social activities requires attention and effort. Drivers must negotiate their attention to the road with their concentration on in-car events. Safety belts may hinder the many side-activities which drivers and other occupants consider to be reasonable and preferable. They are, therefore, conveniently unfastened.

Whenever we are about to participate in any in-car, or for that matter, out-of-car action, we often make some preparatory movements. Unfastening a safety belt is a classic intention movement that displays what we wish to do. For example, conversations in a vehicle may get heated between front-seat and rear-seat passengers. The back-seat occupant takes off the safety belt. This signifies the intent to become more deeply engrossed in talk with other people. The body then aims toward the front seat. The passenger is now in a position to become more bodily involved in a discussion and exerts more authority. Hands and arms can be freely and visibly waved about.

When drivers are about to stop at, for example, a corner store or other facility, they, or their passengers, may be inclined to unfasten their safety belts prior to the arrival at the destination. By doing this they signal the intent to disembark from the vehicle quickly after they have stopped. The rule appears to be that closeness to a destination, coupled by slower speed (e.g., parking lot) and perhaps less traffic, legitimizes unfastening the belt. The fact that a crash may still occur is removed from some people's general thinking mode.

Finally, although not quite as relevant as in past times, lovers may choose to sit close together while the car is moving. The passenger unfastens his or her safety belt and sits closely to the driver. Things lovers do take precedence at the moment.

# CHAPTER 6

# SELF AND OTHERS

# NO PARTICULAR PLACE TO GO

*Riding along in my automobile,*
*My baby beside me at the wheel;*
*I stole a kiss at the turn of a mile,*
*My curiosity running wild.*
*Cruising and playing the radio,*
*With NO PARTICULAR PLACE TO GO.*

*Riding along in my automobile,*
*I was anxious to tell her the way I feel;*
*So I told her softly and sincere,*
*And she leaned and whispered in my ear,*
*Cuddling more and driving slow,*
*With NO PARTICULAR PLACE TO GO.*

*NO PARTICULAR PLACE TO GO,*
*So we parked way out on the cocamo;*
*The night was young and the moon was gold,*
*So we both decided to take a stroll.*
*Can you imagine the way I felt,*
*I couldn't unfasten her **safety belt**.*

*Riding along in my calaboose,*
*Still trying to get her belt unloose,*
*All the way home I held a grudge,*
*For the **safety belt** that wouldn't budge.*
*Cruising and playing the radio,*
*With NO PARTICULAR PLACE TO GO.*
*(emphasis added)*

"NO PARTICULAR PLACE TO GO"

Words and Music by CHUCK BERRY

© Copyright 1964 by ARC MUSIC CORP.
New York, NY   10022.

> Every person lives in a world of social encounters, involving him either in face-to-face or mediated contact with other participants. In each of these contacts, he tends to act out what is sometimes called a "line"—that is, a pattern of verbal and non-verbal acts by which he expresses his view of the situation and through this his evaluation of the participants, especially himself. Regardless of whether a person intends to take a line, he will find that he has done so in effect. The other participants will assume that he has more or less willfully taken a stand, so that if he is to deal with their response to him he must take into consideration the impression they have possibly formed of him (Goffman, 1967, p. 5).

The world in which we all live is composed of manifold relations. Professional, recreational, entrepreneurial, familial, collegial, and legal relationships are but a few we share with others within a common sector of time and space. Within each expressive event we are expected to have self-respect and to sustain a standard of consideration. Through these qualities we effectively claim a certain image with respect to others.

Consider the following formulation derived from Erving Goffman's, *The Presentation of Self in Everyday Life*. When people are in the presence of others, they are interested in managing information about themselves, their feelings, their relationships, their character, their social status, and so forth, which will convey a particular impression to those others. The author elaborates:

> He may wish them to think highly of him, or to think that he thinks highly of them, or to perceive how in fact he feels toward them, or to obtain no clear-cut impression; he may wish to ensure sufficient harmony so that the interaction can be sustained or to defraud, get rid of, confuse, mislead, antagonize, or insult them. Regardless of the particular objective which the individual has in mind and of his motive for having this objective, it will be in his interests to control the conduct of the other, especially their responsive treatment of him. This control is achieved largely by influencing the definition of the situation which the others come to formulate, and he can influence this definition by expressing himself in such a way as to give them the kind of impression that will lead them to act voluntarily in accordance with his own plan (1959, p. 12).

In order to get from others the sort of treatment you want others to give, you must take steps to ensure that they will accept as real your definition of what is important within certain situations. It is in our interests to have persons see us in a particular light, grant us certain identity, and treat us in the way that we consider proper.

Goffman uses the term "the presentation of self" to refer to the techniques that persons employ to get others to see them in a particular way. To a certain extent, the importance of presentation is recognized in everyday discourse: Consider such common expressions as "first impressions," "putting your best foot forward," "getting off on the right foot," and the like.

Driving a vehicle carries with it the need for a smooth social performance. A driver, in the company of passengers, stakes his value in every driving circumstance. His capacity to maintain face in different situations constitutes a display of "savoir faire" (Lyman and Scott, 1970).

Safety belts can play a predominant role in the preservation of a driver's self-concept. Trust and face-saving become measures of behavior. For example, to support drivers' judgments of themselves as competent and reliable, passengers provide them with evidence that this is in fact the case. One motorist who usually wears safety belts as a driver but not as a passenger nicely represented this view shared by many more individuals:

> I trust the people I drive with; they're good drivers. The people I drive with can handle themselves in any situation.

By the same token, a person's image as a competent driver may become tarnished if a passenger wears a safety belt. Some motorists with whom we spoke portrayed their driving character as virtuous and honorable. Passengers are expected to be aware of the driver's attributes or sensitivities. To illustrate:

> I never wear safety belts when I'm with my dad. He doesn't believe in them. If I put them on he accuses me of not trusting his driving and acts hurt. Sometimes my mom puts them on just to get at him.

Consequently, some drivers expect their passengers to maintain trust in their abilities and concern for safety. Their image as good drivers rests on it. So, passengers reinforce the self concept by not wearing a safety belt. Smooth performance of the faith-in-the-driver principle is always unspoken. It is, "One of those things you know you just feel. It's there."

A father, as head of the household, sees himself as responsible. His cultural background reinforces his perception of self. As dependents, other members of the family show respect for his position of responsibility by maintaining a consistent trust. The wearing of a safety belt may be seen as a break in trust. How often do we hear a driver say to a passenger who is buckling up, "What's the matter, don't you trust me?"

The rule of display for self and others based on face-saving can be nicely illustrated with a few more examples. Courtship and dating are widespread institutions in which poise and tact are expected. They require mobilization of moral and social forces to develop into desired long-term relationships. As one young lady so clearly illustrated:

> I usually didn't wear one (safety belt) when I was first going out with my present boyfriend. I felt that if I buckled up and sat on the far side of the car he might see me as being cold and distant. It was a relationship I wanted to continue so I sat over by him.

Indeed, in their accounts concerning courtship some informants suggested that buckling up may be used by some audiences to formulate a self that is not congruent with one's desired projection. A young woman provides an example from a dating situation:

> It was my first date with this guy. He was quite a bit older than me, and I didn't want him to think I was a miss goody-two-shoes so I didn't bother putting my safety belt on.

More extreme, yet prevalent, is the management of a mood through non-use of a safety belt. A short while ago a young man had a single-vehicle fatal accident near a rural village with his half-ton pickup. Events leading up to his death were as follows. He visited his girlfriend to discuss matters of love. A few drinks were consumed while they spoke. Eventually, the lady confirmed his suspicions that she wished to break off the relationship. An argument resulted after which the young man ran to his truck, slammed the door and squealed out, tires smoking. Five miles down the road the fellow met a tree head-on and died. He was not wearing a safety belt. A discussion with his former girlfriend's parents showed that the deceased man usually wore his safety belt. At this time he did not!

Two possible explanations arise. One relates to the fact that anger and emotional turmoil resulting from love affairs are not unusual for either men or women. However, the dramaturgical element of emotions is that they are not only felt but displayed as such. They need to be performed to credit the impression of being highly upset. To jump into his truck, search for his safety belt, fasten it, and then scream out is inconsistent with the characterization which a "deeply hurt" person wishes to display. Therefore, safety belts are only part of the stage-acting, to the extent to which they are not used by design for face. Usage of safety belts at an emotionally stressful time may be incongruent with one's desired projection.

A second viable explanation is that of mood. When a person is in a highly agitated state, his insight and rationality may not be the same as when he is in a normal frame of mind. In the heat of the moment he may judge the wearing of a safety belt as not important in comparison with his topsy-turvy existence at the time. The torn love was the ultimate problem that required attention and thought.

Be cool! A common phrase and one easily recognized in North America. To be cool at the workplace requires the capacity to execute certain physical acts and to show control in risky situations (Lyman and Scott, 1968). A young man personalized Lyman and Scott's social theme with the following account:

> The guys I worked with never wore safety belts so naturally I didn't either. This was whether we were being driven to the site in a van or driving into town on the weekend. It sounds silly but I thought they would kid me about it if I wore one.

Another driver suggests that for a brief period of his life, the persistent non-use of safety belts was needed to display a consistent self:

> When I was about 15, I was going through a sort of rebellious stage. Wearing safety belts like you're supposed to just isn't for rebels, you know. So I never wore them when I was out with my family . . . .

It should be noted that dramaturgical non-use of safety belts is not restricted to occasions when an audience of others is present. As the following example suggests, the significant audience may be oneself:

> It was a fine summer day and I had some good drivin' music on the tapedeck. I felt free like a free spirit. I took the belt off. It didn't go with the image of "me" I had in my mind.

It is proposed then, that for at least some drivers, safety belts are experienced not as morally neutral devices but as morally charged ones whose use or non-use is consequential to the projected self. For them, safety belts are part of the basic sign equipment that can be employed to establish a particular moral character, whether for oneself or others. They are part of an acknowledgment that: I am as the other one sees me (Sartre in Stern, 1967, p. 116).

# CHAPTER 7

# SAFETY BELT NON-WEARING: THE NEIGHBORLY THING TO DO

To exist is to co-exist. To co-exist is to have interplay with others. The others are our contemporaries and among contemporaries, people share a community of time and space. For as Schutz wrote:

> Sharing a community of space implies that a certain sector of the outer world is equally within the reach of each partner and contains objects of common interests and relevance (1973, p. 16).

Toennies (1940) believed that, in communities, individuals not only seek common interests but they also search and find mutual approval and sympathy. A common volition is built around common sets of shared sentiments and attitudes. Individuals become part of a common will, a we-ness, and an inner disposition of spirit.

All major cities have identifiable territorial communities. A tangible one in Vancouver is the Downtown-Eastside. There are a group of people, largely male and senior citizens, who live in hotels on social assistance. In such a community each partner participates in the ongoing life of the other.

The collective life of a geographical community like the Downtown-Eastside is nurtured on the basis of people developing permanent or at least semi-permanent connections to a home. The collection of homes within a visible location represents one kind of a community. In more affluent communities people, through political input, work toward establishing facilities and activities to maintain themselves and strengthen their bonds. Parks, playgrounds, schools and other community facilities are built. Groups, teams and clubs organized on the basis of interests, talents or accomplishments become a significant part of people's neighborhood reality. Picnics, carnivals, fights, weddings, ballgames, funerals and other regional celebrations or frolic events become integral parts of social life. People become involved in vicarious activities which at best the neighborhood encourages and at worst it tolerates.

Another kind of community has no special geographical determinants. It is composed of fellow citizens who may not share a geographical territory but who engage in similar interests and behaviors, or who share similar definitions of reality. Such a community may be individuals in the creative arts (artists and musicians), people sharing certain skills and knowledge (e.g., medical doctors) or persons engaging in similar sexual preferences (e.g., gay communities). Furthermore, biographical qualities of culture, race or ethnicity may serve as community loci.

The person and the community are in a dialectic relationship to one another. The personalities of individual members form the personality of the community. On the other hand, the personality or distinguishing mood of a community reflects the personality of the individuals. For example, some communities like Vancouver's Downtown-Eastside have residents who live close to the edge. Survival depends on people's abilities to steal, shoplift or break into cars. The community may become known for its crime and delinquent action. Its ethos supports criminal acts through the acceptance of individual members. Some residents engage in petty theft because it is an assumed standard of the community. Risk, thereby, becomes a self-community relationship.

In a suburban community of average income earners, it may be quite conventional for a member of the family, say the father, to jump in his car and drive several blocks to the local pub for a few draft beers and a chat with friends and neighbors. Let us further assume that the man does not believe in wearing a safety belt because it is a short trip. His pattern of action may have a structure of familiarity with other community members. The public view of local inhabitants may be such that the father's practices are tolerated, perhaps even endorsed.

Neighbors may see it as a conventional activity consistent with the recreational and leisure standards of the neighborhood. Ordinary citizens will not treat the family man as marginal or as a law breaker because he drove "only" three blocks to "have a few beers" without having his safety belt buckled up. He may be viewed as the father who deserves to do it because he works hard.

Some cultural and religious communities have strong sanctions tied to any one individual breaking the norm of proper conduct. Sikhs are not allowed to remove their knives in public and the Jehovah Witnesses are not permitted to partake of blood transfusions. Similarly, professional communities have a code of ethics by which they must conduct themselves. These examples illustrate that communities take responsibility to control undesired activities.

Other neighborhoods are the product of high-density population and limited space and privacy. According to Berger (1972), such neighborhoods circumscribe recreational functions and create much anxiety and tension. Risk parallels these feelings. In order to survive in such neighborhoods, the inhabitants must take risks. Consequently, increasing risky behavior becomes the norm for citizens. Drinking and driving, safety belt non-wearing, speeding and so on are, within the reference schemes of community actions, considered to be reasonable affairs in a stressful environment.

The cinder-block neighborhoods that condone or even encourage risk-taking tend to be those where members have lower education and socioeconomic standing. In the case of Vancouver's Downtown-Eastside, risk does not carry a conscious decision. According to the Residents' Association:

It's just something you do. It's a risk to live on welfare. To live in a hotel where there's no selection of tenants, where there's problems with tenants next door. In some hotels you can get mugged in the lobby. It's a risk to earn some extra money so welfare won't find out, to steal or shoplift for your kids.

In such communities, personal risk includes living on the edge. You can be thrown out of a hotel at any time without reason, be assaulted in the beer parlor or on the streets, be mugged for anything, or be harassed for reasons of racism or perverted humor.

Fhaner and Hane (1973), Pederson and Mahon (in Jonah and Lawson, 1985), Bragg (1973), and Hannah (1975) concurred in their findings that education and socioeconomic standings were major factors in safety belt wearing. And, of course, these two factors are important definers of people's residency, meaning community. Fear of entrapment, feelings of powerlessness, and assertive feelings arising from anxiety are products of high-density, low-economic status neighborhoods. They are also indicators of safety belt non-wearing.

In our examination of 1,000 British Columbia accident-involved drivers, we calculated the median dwelling-unit income (DUI) for each home postal code. The average dwelling unit incomes were then produced for 500 safety belt wearers and 500 non-wearers, respectively. The median DUI for all drivers was $17,116. The average DUI for safety belt wearers was $17,356, and for non-wearers it was $16,877. The difference was significant at a confidence level of better than 95%. Our results showed a significantly lower economic level (or socioeconomic status) associated with non-wearers than was the case with wearers.

However, in some communities like Vancouver's Downtown-Eastside the average income is only about $10,000 to $12,000. Few people can afford to own cars. In addition, the amount of parking is limited for the community. To own a nice car carries risk. Nice cars would be broken into. The windows, batteries and hub caps would be removed.

So, safety belt wearing is not an everyday relevant item in such communities. Most people either walk, take a bus or occasionally take a taxi. Distances are short. In taxis the residents never use safety belts. They're not in a car very often or for a long period of time.

In all communities there is an assumed rule of conduct. In the Eastside, there is an understanding that certain members of the community should not get ripped off. People would know who ripped off who and would get even. Gossip is shared over coffee in the coffee shop. In the more affluent communities, accepted rules of conduct apply to how inhabitants of the community interact with employees who work there. The emphasis on harmony and accord is vital. The following detailed example illustrates the meaningfulness of such a rule.

Recently, thousands of Lower Mainland British Columbia elementary school children assembled at a local park. There, they would witness the official opening of a playground by the Prince and Princess of Wales for special-needs children. With few exceptions, the children were transported to the park by private vehicles in school-arranged carpools.

When school officials solicited the predominantly "middle class" parents to participate in carpools, they made it clear that for reasons of good sense and safe practice—not to mention the law—each transported child must wear a safety belt. Parents were advised to volunteer to drive only the number of children that they could properly buckle-up. For most schools, this is not merely a suggestion or a recommendation but a policy matter that is taken with extreme seriousness.

On the day of the royal visit, an unknown number of students made the trip either unbuckled or buckled in a way that rendered the restraint ineffective. Under the supervision of teachers, students were assigned to vehicles with an inadequate number of operative safety belts, buckled two to a belt, and permitted to ride in a vehicle's cargo area. Consider the following excerpts from accounts prepared by teachers who witnessed, participated in, or sponsored the making of these unsafe and illegal decisions:

> There were five safety belts all right but only four of them worked. One of them (in the back seat) was hopelessly stuck between the seats. So I buckled the two smallest ones together and we were on our way.

> When you count the driver, there were only three belts available, not four like we thought. She counted wrong . . . one kid kind of scrunched down on the floor in the back.

> It ended up there were three kids in it. Two buckled in the passenger seat and one behind the seats . . . .

Although teachers were specifically told and warned that breach of the safety belt wearing rule could result in injury, death and subsequent litigation, they broke the rule anyway.

At least two explanations of these instances of rule suspension are possible. We could account for it in terms of a defect in the teachers' motivation: They neither cared nor were concerned and, perhaps, are in need of moral or substantive re-education. This explanation can be rejected out of hand. Teachers' comments such as: "I didn't want to do it;" "I didn't feel good about it;" and "What could I do?" suggest that they recognized the generally deviant character of permitting children to travel unrestrained. Their motivation, care and concern were not at issue.

A second explanation assigns these instances of permitted non-compliance to the teachers' interest in preserving routineness in the community and avoiding situational trouble. Before elaborating on this viewpoint, let us begin to document it by examining additional portions of one teacher's account. Consider the following:

> One of the mothers who signed up to drive pulled up in a Corvette. I knew she had this car but I thought she'd bring a different one as they have three. I told her that there weren't enough belts, but she said she always rides with her son or daughter in the back. I didn't want to do it but I thought she'd make a fuss if I pushed her. (She does a lot of volunteer duty around the school.) The kids she was going to drive were best friends of her daughter. It ended up there were three kids in there. Two buckled in the passenger seat and one behind the seats in the window. That's the way she wanted it and that's the way she got it.

It is proposed that this instance of rule-suspension was allowed simply to avoid confrontation within the school-supporting community. From the teacher's point of view, making an issue of it might lead to a dispute involving her, the parent, and the children. Indeed, since the suspension was occasioned by the parent's specific request, she had strong warrant for suspecting that her insistence on adhering to the rule would generate trouble—and, furthermore, trouble that could extend beyond the current situation.

It can be suggested that the teacher is orienting towards the production of a normal state of community affairs and seeking—by her action of permitting the child to ride unbuckled—to guarantee its reproduction. Her suspension can be understood in terms of an interest in getting on with social relationships in a trouble-free manner. From her point of view, standing on principle and thereby denying the parent's request would be contrary to this interest.

It is unknown, of course, whether or not the teacher's insistence that the rule must be followed no matter what would have actually generated the dispute she felt would necessarily transpire. All that is important, however, is her sense that this would be the case. This orientation to presupposed trouble is evident in the following account as well:

> So I buckled the smallest ones together and we were on our way. I didn't feel good about it but what could I do. It was a matter of doing this or leaving the kid behind. I'm not that kind of heartless soul. I could've stayed behind myself, but I was needed to supervise the kids. It was really a case of damned if you do, et cetera. But I was sure to be damned if I stayed behind.

In both the above accounts, it was the actual situation and not the rule to which the teachers were primarily responsive. The rule was reworked and fitted to the situation—not vice versa. Indeed, to paraphrase Garfinkel (1967, p. 13), the actual situation as a phenomenon in its own right exercised an overwhelming priority of relevance to which the rule was subordinated. We can call this "occasional deference."

This heuristic is introduced because the position is taken that teachers, like other people, can be totally aware of the consequences of not using safety belts and be totally committed to ensuring that they are used, and yet still allow interests in smooth social relations within the occasion to "control" their activities. Indeed, deferring to the occasion (the actual situation of choice) is what reasonable people do and are expected to do. Not to do so and to insist that rules be followed in an invariant and trans-situational fashion, could cause one's competence to be called into doubt. The interdependency between people in a neighborhood is then called into question.

The notion of occasional deference explains many more instances of perceived "legitimate" suspensions of the buckle-up rule than just those of the teachers discussed above. Prominent amongst these are adults who routinely and reasonably transport more passengers than safety allows when on outings to movies, to sporting events, and the like.

An extreme case of suspended belief in safety was offered by one driver. The fellow told a story about transporting six nine-year-old girls to and from the waterslides in the back of his pickup truck. The ride was one of the highlights of her birthday party for which his daughter pleaded. "I couldn't disappoint her and it was only a short trip," he reasoned.

In a series of interviews, time and time again motorists described situations where they had permitted more passengers than there were safety belts in order to lessen the risk of social animosity or repercussion. One said that she was involved for two years in a carpool that always had one more child than belts. There were seven children in the pool. Four always sat in the back. To do the carpool with one less family would have increased her driving time considerably and would have left one family "out in the cold."

The woman stated that at no time did she feel guilty about transporting more children than the available number of safety belts would allow. Furthermore, she said that she never considered installing an extra safety belt. Other interviewees who were present agreed. They also would not have bothered. They justified their views by turning to the 'back seat is safer' argument outlined in chapter 4.

To gain greater insight into the driver's reasoning, the speaker was asked, "knowing what she knew now, would she carry yet another child in her carpool?" Without hesitation, she answered that if it would reduce the number of times she had to drive to and from school, she would. Even without a safety belt! She told the researcher that he did not know what it was like to drive children back and forth to school. "Even with a carpool it ruins your day," she said. She further divulged that she had occasionally transported more than two unbuckled children in her car. One of her friends—a single parent—works shift and sometimes has trouble arranging for her son's transportation to school. She has a carpool, "but it doesn't always work out because she doesn't do her share." She said that she "has to" drive her friend's son because of friendship obligations. Other participants defended her and noted that they would do the same thing. Retaining proper relationships with friends and neighbors was a part of a social code which requires full adherence by members.

To promote discussion, the group leader spoke about a colleague who refused to transport a child home from a Cub Scout meeting because he did not have safety belts for more than the scheduled number of children. Participants were in uniform agreement that this was carrying a principle too far. "What do you do, just leave the kid there," one member asked rhetorically. None of the drivers advised us that they would feel uncomfortable about transporting an unrestrained child under the circumstances. The discussion leader continued to play the devil's advocate. He suggested that we are living in a litigation-happy society:

> "What if there was an accident," he asked, "and the unrestrained child was severely injured. Would the parents shake your hand and thank you for driving him home?" "But there wouldn't be an accident," participants responded. One gentleman had done "something like that" when his son was playing soccer. "There were always kids that needed rides home after the game," he said. He thought nothing of it. "Why were you sure there wouldn't be an accident?" asked the author. "It was only a short drive," he stated.

To have friends and neighbors and to keep proper relations with them require obligations that must be met. Some of the obligations expose people to certain physical risks. However, the physical risk is considered on an empirical or rational basis. The social risk of accentuating possible situations whereby a relationship may be seen to become defective is considered to be of primary importance. As Durkheim wrote:

> The human personality is a sacred thing; one does not violate it nor infringe its bounds, while at the same time, the greatest good is in communion with others (1953, p. 37).

The predominant belief in keeping social ties, thought to be legitimate by many people in our society, may, however, be questioned by "experts." Flirting with and indulging in risky behavior such as safety belt non-wearing are open for analysis by traffic safety researchers.

In our 1986 sample of 1,000 British Columbia accident-involved drivers, a total of 19 cases were identified where the vehicle driven was carrying more occupants than there were saftey belts available. In 17 (90%) of these cases, the driver was unbelted. Given that only about 20 percent or so of drivers in the general population of British Columbia drivers are unbelted at any given time, this result is very meaningful. Obviously these drivers, as the vehicle occupants most legally responsible and most able to exercise control over the social situations, were not, as our previously quoted interviewees described, likely caught in an ethical, legal or social dilemma. Ignoring well-known rules governing the carrying of unbelted passengers was more likely a function of their own non-belief in the efficacy of safety belts or the legitimacy of safety belt legislation.

# CHAPTER 8

# SAVING YOU FROM YOURSELF, OR SAVING SOCIETY FROM YOU

**"How do you plead to the charge of speeding?"**

# Introduction

Law "is nothing else than an ordinance of reason for the common good, made by him who has care of the community." (Aquinas, p. 995)

As members of society we insist on making distinctions between our public and private lives. We recognize the need to be governed but do not necessarily consent to having our private judgments subordinated to public judgments. A convenient illustration concerns the issue of the bedroom. Societal members resent having their private affairs become determined by a political caucus. Or as the past Canadian Prime Minister Pierre Trudeau said, "The state has no business in the bedrooms of the nation." We criticize and condemn as "totalitarian" any government which fails to distinguish the public from the private (Tussman, 1979).

All members of an electorate have a unique yet general relation to the government. They are private persons who elect officials—who in turn design public laws which govern the electors' behaviors. The laws become the products of a social contract between the government and the people. Fagothey (1976) provided an in-depth description of laws, ethics and practice. His five strategic components of law provide the framework for any discussion on safety belt laws and safety belt wearing:

1. A law is called an ordinance because it is no mere advice, counsel, or suggestion but an order, a command, and a mandate imposing the superior's will on the inferior's and binding with moral necessity.

2. A law is said to be of reason because it must be no arbitrary whim but intelligent direction, imposed by the superior's will but planned and formulated by right reason. To be reasonable a law must be consistent with other laws and rights, just in distributing benefits and burdens, observable as not being too harsh or difficult, enforceable so that proper observation is actually secured, and useful in that the good it aims at is worth the price.

3. A law is for the common good, for the welfare of the community as a whole, and not for the benefit of individuals as such. A command authoritatively given to an individual about a private matter can require his obedience but is not a law.

4. A law must be promulgated, or made known to those whom it binds. It must be published in such a manner that it can be known readily, though each subject need not be given personal notice.

5. A law must come from one who has care of the community, from a legislator having authority or jurisdiction, who may be a single individual or a body passing laws by joint action. Not anyone who pleases may pass a law. What sets the lawgiver off from the rest and gives him the right to command is his authority (1976, p. 109).

Unfortunately Fagothey's eloquent definition of laws is dissimilar to the social process of law. When legal minds present "the judicial process," they refer to the style and logic of court decisions (Gusfield, 1981). They speak past the cultural dimension of law—the acts of police, lawyers, judges and courts.

In the case of safety belt use, the mandatory safety belt law is not a specific reaction to a particular person. It is a statute that presents a face of universality, reason and certainty. It gives no indication of particularism, uniqueness of events, and negotiation in which drivers, police, attorneys and courts act (Gusfield, 1981). Nevertheless, these may be present. As one interviewed driver explained, one's chances of getting ticketed for non-use are minimal—the RCMP detachment that is responsible in his home area is small and is too busy to worry about whether citizens are buckled up. In conjunction with this latter reason, he noted that rural law enforcement is "more personal" and if non-use was detected you would probably be "let off" rather than be ticketed.

Yet the same motorist "always" wears his safety belts when he visits relatives in the urban Lower Mainland of British Columbia. Besides having a perceived greater risk of an accident there than at home, he feels that his chances of being caught are greater because "there are more police around."

Safety belt wearing laws posit a public standard of behavior and present it as an acceptable canon of society. According to Gusfield:

Law, like other forms of public action, becomes a part of public, societal culture. It is a presentation of a patterned, stereotyped, and abstract set of criteria presented as the perspective of "society" functioning in a collective capacity. That collectivity is itself a fiction, created and reinforced in the public act of its presentation (1981, p. 144).

# A Law For Everyone

Doubts about the uniformity of behavior underlying society are sometimes raised by motorists. For example, one gentleman participating in our group discussions stated that recently he had seen "the odd bus driver" putting on safety belts when taking over the bus.

He wanted to know if this was required. Discussion focussed on the commonly expressed concern that for certain categories of operators—such as taxi drivers, bus drivers and delivery personnel—safety belt use might be legally optional. Special mention was made of some mailmen who "never seem to be wearing one," even though they often drive with their doors open. Such exceptions were noted as making an impact on even the most casual observer. Another driver stated, "You hardly ever see a cop wearing one so why should I." The fairness of leaving optional to some what is mandatory to others was a pressing question. The notion that safety belt use might impede a person's work did little to settle those who felt that "what is good for the goose is good for the gander." Participants felt that the police, as moral examples, should be required to wear safety belts: "It's hypocritical to have them go into schools and talk about safety when they don't follow the rules of safety themselves." Common agreement with this point of view was documented.

Everyday logic has it that if the law is good, all people must abide by it. If certain groups are exempt from the law, the law is not universal. If there are exemptions it cannot be just. If it is not just it does not need to be obeyed. A rationale is therefore constructed for non-adherence to the safety belt law. Moreover, in the strict sense, it is the law which is irrational. In British Columbia, for example, drivers engaged in work requiring frequent boarding and alighting and where travel speeds do not exceed 40 km/h are excluded from the requirement to wear belts. Yet such conditions, as we have seen, do not guarantee freedom from accident risk. In this case, a law, promoted on the basis of individual safety for the common good, permits exemption on the basis of convenience. A similar situation would occur if provisions of the new *National Safety Code* driver standards were proposed to be not applicable to certain classes of operators (such as farmers) for mainly economic reasons. If the legislative rationale is valid, why can the law be circumvented for reasons outside such rationale? Even though the reasons may appear quite logical, the inconsistency must reduce the law's credibility.

# Avoiding Sanctions

For many people, safety belt wearing is done not because of safety but because of the law. A point of clarification is required. People who wear safety belts because of the law may not do so because of their belief in the legitimacy of the edict, but rather because of their duty to avoid sanctions if they are caught breaking the law. This was noted as a general rule of thought.

Some motorists characterized police enforcement of the safety belt law as "a waste of time" and an inappropriate deployment of resources. Somewhat in defence of police activity, however, was the opinion that roadblocks are "the only way they're going to get people to wear safety belts." Otherwise, "most people wouldn't bother wearing them." Our researcher feigned disbelief and indicated that he thought just the opposite: that these days most people wear safety belts out of a concern for safety, not because of fear of a fine. The view that most people wear a safety belt because of the police was too cynical. The interviewer was accused of being naive:

> "People don't wear safety belts because they believe they will save their lives," one participant said. "They wear them because they have to. Who wants to pay a $35 fine."

A prominent theme that arose time and time again was that if the safety belt law were repealed, a significant number of motorists would stop buckling up. As described throughout this manuscript, too many people have too many reasons for not wearing safety belts.

A common judicial argument for penalties and sanctions is to deter future lawbreakers. In British Columbia, non-compliance with the safety belt wearing law calls for a $35.00 fine. Some motorists said that the fine was "obviously" no deterrent for them, since they just pay it and continue to drive unrestrained. The fine was translated as an "inconvenience" that people could "live with." One gentleman noted that if the fine were raised to an amount that "hurt," say, for example, 100 or 150 dollars, he would probably resort to wearing safety belts more often. The frowns on the faces of his colleagues showed a great deal of displeasure with the idea, so he went further to conclude that safety belt wearing was essentially a waste of time and effort. It was a commonly held view that a severe penalty "for such a small thing" would be unfair.

# Fairness of a Mandatory Safety Belt Law

It was not unusual to find that many safety belt wearers and non-wearers alike questioned the authenticity of the mandatory safety belt wearing legislation in British Columbia. People continue to debate why they "must" wear safety belts, when according to them, "the evidence that safety belts prevent or reduce injury is still a little iffy." They are not like faulty brakes, which if they were not legislated against, could be seen definitely to cause accidents.

The critical perspective on fairness can best be illustrated by featuring people's own versions. One participant said that he thought it was "unfair and hypocritical" that the government forces people to wear safety belts when it permits people to engage in many other things that are hazardous to their health—like smoking and drinking, and even allowing the operation of a car at the "tender" age of sixteen. If the government were rational in its concern for citizens, he noted, it would extend rationality to more areas of social life. Although he wears his safety belt to avoid a fine, he removes it when he drives in parts of North America where there are no mandatory safety belt wearing laws.

The pervasive argument of unfair legislation took several turns. One driver characterized himself as "free and over 21." He believed that he should be allowed to do whatever he wants, even if it does involve a degree of risk. Though he regularly wore safety belts he felt that it should be a matter of choice, not a legal requirement. He noted that this is especially the case when the benefits of use are as much a matter of opinion as fact. The gentleman noted that the government allows people to choose to take chances in domains that are much more dangerous than traffic. He cited the recent high number of deaths amongst rafters on British Columbia white-water rivers. Would the government consider legislation making all rafters wear appropriate protective head and body gear? A similar question concerned the issue that bicyclists or even skateboarders are not required to wear helmets by law like motorcyclists. An answer to this question is difficult. Obviously it is impossible for the government to attempt to reduce all risks. True, replied interviewees, but there are other areas that could be looked into. One motorist noted, sarcastically, that if governments found out that tourists were avoiding certain provinces or states because they had to wear safety belts, they would abolish mandatory safety belt use immediately. The principle that economics supersedes safety was considered to be paramount when it concerned government priorities.

What would happen if the government had used a plebiscite rather than a fiat to decide whether safety belts should be mandatory? "It would've never gotten through," said one motorist. Another added that "even now" passage would be unlikely "if the people had anything to say about it." General support for the answers was evident. The interviewer feigned incredulity and asked how it could be possible that the populace would reject a measure that was of obvious benefit to the community. He was continuously reminded that his sense of what is beneficial is not necessarily consistent with everyone else's. It's a matter of perspective. "There's lots of people," said one interviewee, "who think safety belts are dangerous." He told a story of a co-worker who was ticketed for non-use. The non-use was not deliberate, he'd merely forgotten to buckle up. According to the respondent the colleague:

Went on and on about the unfairness of being fined for not wearing them when nobody's sure if they do any good in the first place. Think how that cop would've felt if I'd had an accident and got trapped in my car.

The point was made that this person is not an adamant, committed non-user, or one who has an axe to grind. He was portrayed as an "ordinary" person who wears safety belts primarily because he "has to." Like most people though, "he has his doubts" about the effectiveness of buckling up. The general opinion was expressed that a survey would reveal "most people" to have an opinion of safety belts ranging from neutral to dangerous in terms of what they will do for you in the event of a collision. Equally evident was the thought that some people do not wear their safety belts because they believe that the law does not accurately reflect the limited danger of non-wearing.

Our detailed interviews with observed safety belt wearers and non-wearers led us to conclude that most drivers, whether usual restraint users or non-users, apparently favor, or at least accept, the legislation of safety belt wearing. The predominant reason given was that belts enhance safety. The slightly less than half of non-wearers who were against legislation usually cited individual rights as their reason for opposition.

Overall, the majority of the interviewed drivers also felt that fines were a legitimate form of safety belt use control. Again, only slightly less than half of the observed non-wearers disagreed with this premise but even those who supported fines felt that they should be low in value ($25 or less were favored by most). The great majority of our surveyed drivers (over three-quarters), however, considered the chances of being caught and fined as low. This was so for both observed wearers and non-wearers alike.

# CHAPTER 9

# DO SAFETY BELTS
# REDUCE INJURY?

"You're lucky you were wearing your seatbelt."

In the last eight chapters we spent considerable time explaining legitimate views held by people on the appropriateness of safety belt non-wearing for certain social or vehicular occasions. We described at length people's views on safety belts' attenuating or accentuating the risk of injury. Most of the commonsense deliberations were based on beliefs and assumptions people held as laypersons. Now it is time to view the matter from another perspective—one based on rigorous analysis and empirical reasoning.

How effective are safety belts in reducing injury severity? The concept that vehicle occupants can more readily withstand the forces in an impact if they can take advantage of the energy-absorbing properties of the chassis is well known. Racing car drivers have long profited from such a notion and belts were early-on adopted as a requirement in this sport. We should also be well aware of the usefulness of safety belts in keeping one in place during emergency maneuvers. We are required to wear them every time we fly in an aircraft.

The problem is that most people see flying and automobile racing as special events—high speed and high risk—even though airplane travel is far safer than car driving on a per-kilometre basis. Modern, sanctioned automobile racing is remarkably free of death or serious injury in spite of the apparent dangers. Such activities are seen as not comparable, and their precautions thus not applicable, to low-speed driving on city or suburban streets.

Speed is certainly an important factor in accident-injury probability. The probability of a young or middle-aged person being significantly injured in a crash when traveling at, say, 15 km/h is not high even for unbelted occupants. This probability rises very quickly, however, with increasing speed. By 60 km/h, a typical travel speed for the majority of cars in urban/suburban situations, an unrestrained occupant is very likely to suffer some form of injury. But the fact that some people are not apparently injured and some of them suffer only minor injuries, which may be "brushed-over" in the telling, leaves room for the growth of a mythology within the minds of those predisposed to believe it. Further, this mythology has for many years been fueled by television representations of car crashes where the unbelted occupants crawl unscathed from their demolished cars or else they are "thrown-free" and left unhurt. At the far end of the scale (e.g., crash speeds of over 100 km/h) where damage intrudes into the occupant compartment, the effectiveness of belts will certainly begin to decrease. Such high-speed crashes, however, form only a very small proportion of all accidents.

Another factor in injury severity, and also one that influences the effectiveness of safety belts, is the direction of impact. In accordance with Newton's laws of motion, unrestrained occupants in a vehicle will effectively "move" in the direction of the origin of the force—that is, toward the impacted area (actually, the impacted area moves towards them). The area of the vehicle interior toward which the person is directed can be critical in determining the resultant injuries. Steering wheels, windshields, door handles and rear view mirrors—all may become lethal instruments. Even when restrained, certain collision configurations are more hazardous than others. Side impacts are not as effectively countered by lap/shoulder belts as are frontal impacts for which the restraints are primarily designed. Luckily, for those who wear safety belts, side impacts form a distinct minority of vehicle damage configurations. In an examination of over 125,000 damaged vehicles we found less than one-quarter (21%) to have suffered damage to the side of the occupant compartment. At least with safety belts, there is a significant measure of protection afforded in cases where the impact occurs on the opposite side of the vehicle from where the occupant is sitting. The lap portion of the restraint prevents the person from being thrown across the compartment.

What about the vehicle itself? Does bigger mean safer? The answer, in a general sense, is yes. This is for two reasons. First, another aspect of Newtonian mechanics decrees that energy transfer is a function of mass as well as speed. Simply put, if a big car runs head-on into a small car, the latter will come off worse. Secondly, larger cars usually have longer hoods (engine compartments) in front of them and bigger trunks behind. These areas provide space for energy-absorbing deformation in the event of a crash. Less collision energy is transferred to the occupant compartment to be experienced as injury-resulting acceleration by occupants. Such a situation works to your advantage even if your opponent is a concrete wall.

Finally, there is the question of occupant age. Young persons in the prime of life can often recover well from even serious trauma whereas a similar injury might result in death for an older person. Elderly people also have a skeletal structure which is less resilient and they are therefore more prone to suffer fractures for a given level of applied force.

All of the above factors—speed, impact direction, vehicle size, occupant age and seating position—must be taken into account when assessing safety belt effectiveness. Our data set of 1,000 accident-involved drivers allowed us to control for all of these factors.

We were able to assess approximate crash speed from the speed limit applicable to the accident site, and from extent of damage and repair cost data using a model developed at the University of British Columbia. This model examined the relationships between impact speed, extent of car body deformation and repair cost. The result was a method to estimate collision speed based on vehicle repair cost and value.

We obtained vehicle weight from insurance files, and both driver age and area of major vehicle damage from the Motor Vehicle Department accident database. For each of the drivers in our data set who were taken (but not necessarily admitted) to hospital, we hand-searched the insurance files to arrive at the type and severity of injury. An Abbreviated Injury Scale (AIS) value was then assigned using the United States Department of Transport coding guidelines. We then purged the names of the victims and all other identifying variables prior to constructing the final database. There was no way left to recreate the association of injury to specific victim, and thus anonymity was maintained.

The Abbreviated Injury Scale is a six-point severity scale first developed in 1971 by a joint committee of the American Medical Association, the American Association for Automotive Medicine, and the Society of Automotive Engineers. It came into widespread use by crash investigators with the publication of the AIS Manual in 1976. The AIS scale is used to rate each injury a victim receives in terms of its potential to result in death. An AIS value of 1 represents minor injuries such as bruises and abrasions whereas 6 is a fatal injury. For a given victim, we use the term ''Maximum AIS'' (MaxAIS) to refer to the AIS rating of the most severe injury he or she sustained.

In the following presentation of results, mean values of MaxAIS are given with decimal places, even though the AIS scale is made up of discrete numbers from 1 to 6. This can be seen as similar to the situation of rolling a die which has discrete face values of 1 to 6 but where the expected (long-term average) value of a single roll is 3.5 (the sum of the numbers on the faces, divided by six)—a number which obviously cannot actually be obtained.

We performed a multiple-regression analysis using MaxAIS as the dependent variable. In other words, we wanted to find out which of the recorded driver/vehicle characteristics were significant factors influencing the subsequent level of driver injury. The multiple regression process allowed us to tell which variables were important in ''predicting'' MaxAIS independent of their relationship with other variables. To employ a somewhat frivolous analogy for the purpose of illustration, one might ask: is the sale of umbrellas related to the occurrence of vehicle skidding or is it just that during wet weather (when skidding on slippery pavements can occur) people are more predisposed toward buying umbrellas? Looking only at umbrella sales and skidding accidents we might be tempted to postulate a relationship but we would, of course, be wrong in this assumption. A multiple regression analysis would tell us that umbrella sales are not related to accidents independent of the other variable (i.e., weather).

Variables that were significantly related to driver injury at the 99% level of confidence and their relationships with MaxAIS were:

- Impact configurations involving the top of the vehicle produced greater injury (i.e., likely roll situations).
- The wearing of safety belts resulted in lesser injury.
- Higher collision speeds produced greater injury.

Other variables included in the analysis were driver age, vehicle weight and driver sex but none of these were significant contributors to injury level variance at even the 95% confidence level.

As we anticipated, vehicle weight was inversely related to injury (i.e., heavier vehicles were associated with lesser injuries) although the level of association was not high enough for significance in relation to the other variables considered. On a univariate basis, the mean MaxAIS level for heavy vehicles (over 2,000 kg) was 0.28, while that for light vehicles (under 1,000 kg) was 0.54. This difference was not quite significant at the 95% confidence level.

Similarly, driver age demonstrated an association with MaxAIS, but one which was below the standard of significance in a multivariate analysis. The major effect appeared to be for elderly drivers, age 56 and older, for whom injury levels tended to be higher, especially at greater speeds. For example, the mean MaxAIS level for age 56+ drivers in higher speed collisions was 1.77, while that for the youngest group (ages 16 to 18) was 0.88. The foregoing difference was not significant owing to the relatively small data cell sizes.

There is considerable uncertainty associated with the variable values employed in the foregoing analysis. The problems of defining safety belt use have already been discussed, but certainly the least accurate estimation involved that of collision speed. It was for this reason that speed was resolved into a simple categorical variable represented by three levels: lower, middle and higher. Nominally, these three categories were defined by estimated impact speed ranges of $\leq$ 20 km/h, 21 to 35 km/h, and $\geq$ 36 km/h, respectively but, since each individual estimate was subject to an error ranging up to 100%, broad categorizations were the only justifiable approach. It should be noted that we have assumed impact speeds to be only about 1/2 to 3/4 of average travel speeds; this is to account for some braking of the vehicles prior to collision. Since the estimation of speed was used for rough categorization purposes only, no attempt was made to calculate such things as "equivalent barrier speeds" or actual speed change for each vehicle during a crash. The absolute value of the estimated speeds is thus not important as long as the three-level categorization is reasonably reliable in a qualitative or comparative sense.

Another difficulty had to do with the sample size. The necessity to hand-search files for injury information restricted the overall sample which, in turn, made it necessary to use broad categories for all variables. The side impact situation includes driver and passenger side damage records, and the driver age was classified in five levels. The sensitivity of the effects on injury level may thus be somewhat reduced. Otherwise, non-significance of MaxAIS differences was primarily a consequence of small sample sizes (e.g., predominantly rear-end damage situations were too infrequent to assess confidently).

Accuracy and sensitivity problems undoubtedly were a large part of the reason why the combined contribution of all the applicable variables only explained about 30% of the observed variation in MaxAIS. Even including the extent of vehicle damage (an estimated vehicle deformation index based on a police-assigned code which was entirely independent of the damage data used to estimate speed) did not produce much improvement. It was relatively highly correlated with collision speed level and this at least lent some credence to our speed categorization. Figure 2 shows the relationship among speed, vehicle damage and injury severity for belted and unbelted drivers.

**Figure 2**
**Driver Injury, Vehicle Speed and Deformation**

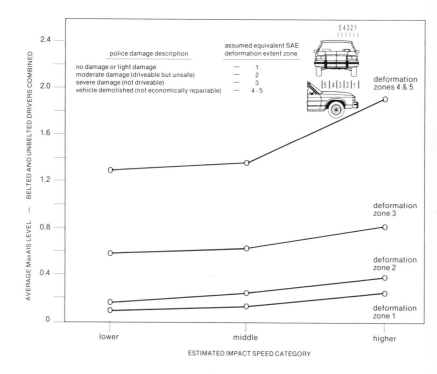

Even considering the high levels of uncertainty involved with some of the data, there is another conclusion which is unavoidable. That is, under virtually all crash conditions there is a wide range of consequences even for unbelted occupants—from no injury up to death. One only has to examine the average MaxAIS levels associated with different speed and impact configurations to realize this. As figure 3 shows, although the use of safety belts clearly and significantly reduced the average injury levels in most situations, the mean MaxAIS values, even for those unrestrained, are low.

For example, unbelted drivers in vehicles which probably rolled (top damage in combination with other areas) at a relatively high speed averaged about 2 on a MaxAIS scale of 1 to 6. An examination of the MaxAIS distribution for these drivers showed that 40% suffered only minor injuries and 13% apparently had no injuries worth treating. As mentioned at the beginning of this chapter, it is the not-insignificant likelihood of such benign consequences which gives the anecdotal evidence adopted by non-wearers the illusion of credence to them. Yes, it is possible to survive, relatively unscathed, a high-speed crash if you are unbelted but the odds are not very good. You will need all of the luck that our interviewed subjects in Chapter 4 put their trust in!

**Figure 3**
**Effectiveness of Lap/Shoulder Restraints**
**(MaxAIS Levels)**

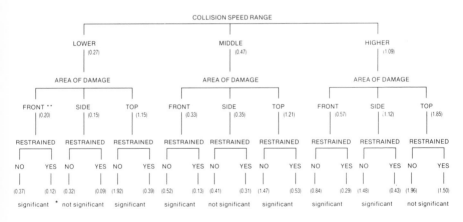

---

\* In student's "t" test on normalized MaxAIS values.
\*\* The majority resulting from rear-end crashes.
  (Where no injury was reported, AIS was assumed to be 0)

The results of our analysis were unequivocal in their direction. Safety belts do reduce injuries. Figure 4 clearly demonstrates this in the case of frontal impacts which was the predominant damage configuration and the situation for which belts were primarily designed. Even in side impacts—which included driver's side damage—we found evidence of reduced severity with safety belts, especially at higher impact speeds. In addition, the ability of safety belts to keep a driver in place, and especially inside the vehicle, was amply proven. In probable roll situations, 28% of 122 unbelted drivers were either fully or partially ejected with an average MaxAIS of 2.32—the highest level for any driver grouping. In similar situations, none of 48 belted drivers was ejected and their average MaxAIS was 0.81.

**Figure 4**
**Effectiveness of Safety Belts in Frontal Impacts**

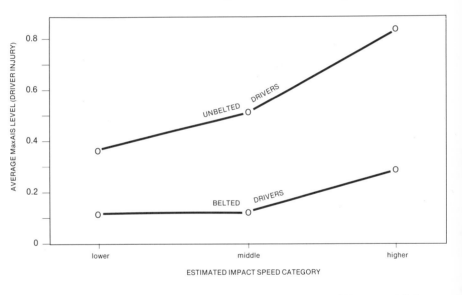

Finally, since the next chapter concerns different driving characteristics of usual wearers vs. usual non-wearers, it is interesting to note that the 122 non-wearers involved in the roll-over crashes—which are often associated with loss of control at higher speeds—represented one-quarter of all non-wearing drivers. In comparison, less than 7% of belt wearers was involved in such situations. In spite of the invalidity of absolute categorization with respect to full-time belt use or non-use, it appears that there may be certain driving-related characteristics which attach themselves more frequently to those who most often do not wear them than to those who most often do. The next chapter will explore this thesis.

# CHAPTER 10

# ARE SAFETY BELT NON-WEARERS DIFFERENT FROM WEARERS?

# Introduction

We have previously seen that general categorization of drivers into safety belt wearers and non-wearers is an oversimplification and tends to hide a number of important aspects of everyday social or moral choice. Nevertheless, our surveys and interviews clearly indicated that there are those, on one end of the scale, who almost never wear belts and those, at the other end, who almost always wear them.

It might be expected that these two groups of people would have greatly differing views, not only on safety belts and safety belt legislation but also on a variety of traffic safety and law enforcement topics. Further, based on previous research concerning different characteristics of those who voluntarily choose to wear or not to wear safety belts, we could anticipate that those drivers who—even in the face of sanctions—choose not to buckle up may display behaviors different from frequent restraint users.

# Accident Involvement Risk

Such speculation as presented above initially focuses on accident risk. The previous chapter dealt with the increased chance of injury for unbelted drivers in a crash. However, do drivers who refuse to buckle up tend to become involved in more accidents in the first place? This is a question not of safety belt effectiveness but of driver attitudes and behaviors—the propensity of some drivers to cause accidents due to certain characteristics, of which safety belt non-wearing is only symptomatic. In such cases, restraint non-use is simply a surrogate for a whole class of attitudes and behaviors. It, like accidents, is an outcome.

One way to examine this is to employ the "odds ratio" technique. Figure 5 illustrates a 2 x 2 matrix of frequencies or probabilities for accident-involved drivers. If belt non-wearers are more likely to be at fault in accidents than belt wearers, then the ratio of $n_{11} n_{22} / n_{12} n_{21}$ will be greater than one.

**Figure 5**
**Probabilities of Accident-Involved Drivers**

|  | Not at fault | At fault |
|---|---|---|
| **Wearing belt** | $n_{11}$ | $n_{12}$ |
| **Not wearing belt** | $n_{21}$ | $n_{22}$ |

There are, of course, a number of different ways in which fault/no fault can be assumed and also several ways of estimating belt wearing. Using insurance and police records for single- and two-vehicle crashes attended by police, we constructed a fault decision flow diagram as indicated in figure 6.

**Figure 6**
**Fault Decision Flow Diagram**

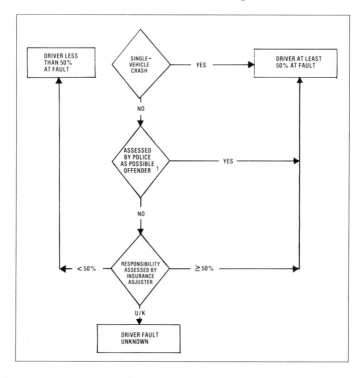

From other studies at the Insurance Corporation (Cooper, 1985), we know that reported safety belt wearing, even in police-attended accidents, is overrepresented in British Columbia. Legal sanctions and past court-assigned assessments of contributory negligence have made people wary of admitting to safety belt non-use. In cases where the police recorded that belts were not worn, they represented either instances where the driver or occupant admitted being unrestrained or else the evidence for such was relatively clear-cut.

---

[1] There is a specific code on the police accident form for this purpose. Such an assessment is often, but not necessarily, supported by the laying of charges. The police only assign a possible offender designation to about 30% of drivers, which implies that the evidence must be reasonably strong.

Defining cases of actual use is more difficult. At the police report level, these data are distorted by a significant group of non-wearers. One way to eliminate some of these possible misrepresenters is to also require a past driving record clear of safety belt non-wearing offences. To be even more certain of belt use, we could additionally require that the driver had suffered no (or only minor) injuries in a crash which resulted in significant vehicular damage.

We used the above definitions of belt use and accident fault or responsibility to generate values for the 2 x 2 matrix from two years of accident data. The values for each cell are shown in figure 7.

## Figure 7
### Safety Belt Wearing/Non-Wearing vs. Fault Conditions

**Safety belt wearing definition No. 1**
**(wearing in accident and with no prior convictions)**

|  | Not at fault | At fault |
|---|---|---|
| **Wearing** | 15,530 | 20,584 |
| **Not wearing** | 712 | 2,340 |
| TOTAL | 16,242 | 22,924 |

**Safety belt wearing definition No. 2**
**(wearing in accident, no prior convictions and minor injuries in a serious crash)**

|  | Not at fault | At fault |
|---|---|---|
| **Wearing** | 2,576 | 4,284 |
| **Not wearing** | 712 | 2,340 |
| TOTAL | 3,288 | 6,624 |

The odds ratios ($R = n_{11}n_{22}/n_{12}n_{21}$) are as follows:

$R_1 = 2.48$      (Standard error = 0.11)
$R_2 = 1.98$      (Standard error = 0.10)

The lower ratio associated with the more stringent definition of safety belt wearing probably means that the increased efficiency of identification is more than offset by the involvement of these drivers in more severe accidents. This latter factor likely favors more frequent "at fault" assessments.

Regardless of the restraint-wearing definition, however, the results are quite similar. Those drivers not buckling-up are distinctly more at risk of accident causation although, of course, this has nothing to do with safety belts per se.

So, one of the characteristics of drivers who refuse to buckle up appears to be that they are involved in more than their fair share of accidents. Are there other identifiable characteristics which distinguish them from those who usually do wear belts? The next section addresses this question.

# Descriptive Results of an Observational and Interview Survey

Our survey of safety belt wearers and non-wearers, as defined by observation, was intended to explore evident differences between these two groups. By requiring that individual driver use or non-use be registered either on high-speed highways or else on two successive days in urban areas, we felt reasonably comfortable in being able to apply our generalized definitions of wearers (frequent users) and non-wearers (infrequent users). Obviously, there is some degree of crossover between highway and city groups—some who never wear in the city may wear on the highway—nevertheless, we still had two largely different, if somewhat indistinct, groupings. At any rate, this was more reliable than simply using a single observation at urban/suburban locations, which is the procedure followed in most restraint use surveys.

Webb et al. (1988) have documented the problems of using self-reported restraint wearing behavior as a means of reliably classifying wearers and non-wearers. They also found that single observations of adult belt use in an urban setting were not reliable indicators of "usual" restraint status.

The results of the survey were matched with driver records by the Motor Vehicle Department who then destroyed all identifying data elements. The file we received was thus purged of any information which could lead to driver identification. The survey methodology and a copy of the questionnaire used are contained in the Appendices. A total of 380 drivers was observed (273 safety belt wearers and 107 non-wearers). Interviews were conducted with 239 (63%) of the drivers.

## Survey demographics

During the survey we attempted to match observed wearers and non-wearers by age and gender categories. This was largely successful: 58.6%

of wearers were males as were 58.9% of non-wearers; 7.0% of wearers were 25 years of age or less as were 8.4% of non-wearers; 39.6% of wearers were age 26-40 as were 43.0% of non-wearers; 19.8% of wearers were age 41-55 as were 19.6% of non-wearers; and 33.7% of wearers were over 55 years of age as were 29.0% of non-wearers. Thus, univariate comparisons between observed wearers and non-wearers should at least be free of age and gender effects. The only noteworthy feature is the almost total absence of drivers under the age of 18. This is because students in high school parking lots were not sampled.

Other demographic variables described were marital status and income level. While the overall marital status distributions between observed wearers and non-wearers were not significantly different, there was a significantly higher percentage of single persons in the non-wearing group (**46.5%** vs. **29.2%** for wearers). In subsequent descriptions we will express significance in terms of the results of the non-parametric chi-square test, where the observed number of wearers and non-wearers in a given category are compared to the expected values based on the overall sample proportion in that category. Differences between observed wearers and non-wearers, which are significant on this basis at the 5% level or better, are printed in **bold** type and shown to one decimal place.

Where drivers reported being currently employed, the observed non-wearers had a greater representation in the lower income brackets (under $30,000 per year)—**61.4%** vs. **42.9%** for wearers.

## Other driver and vehicle characteristics

The overall distributions of driving experience were quite similar between observed wearers and non-wearers, although the former was skewed somewhat more towards high experience levels (25 years or more).

In terms of the vehicle driven, there was a slight tendency for the observed non-wearers to be driving cars of lower value then the wearers but the difference was not significant. Of more significance was the fact that non-wearers were more likely to be driving vehicles over 10 years old (**22.0%** of non-wearers vs. **7.3%** of wearers) although there was no evident difference in the proportion of newer cars (i.e., $\leq$ 5 years old).

The type of insurance policy (rate class) was of interest for those drivers observed on two successive occasions entering downtown parking lots. While such activity would not be precluded under a "pleasure-only" premium unless they had driven to work more than four days during the month, nevertheless those apparently driving to work two days in a row and who were insured only for pleasure driving may be considered as possibly mis-rated. Mis-rating, of course, essentially means being knowingly (for most) underinsured. The driver balances the premium saving against his estimate of the risk of having an accident for which he may not be covered. As we have seen previously, past research has suggested a link between safety belt wearing and the purchase of insurance.

In fact, 80% of the applicable drivers were rated for driving to or from work. The observed non-wearers had an ''incorrect'' rating level of 25% as opposed to that for the wearers of 18%. The difference was not significant, however, owing to the small sample size involved.

## General driving characteristics

One of the most important aspects of driving is the quantity of exposure. Here we found that the observed non-wearers apparently drove more often (or for longer durations) than the wearers. Over 28% of non-wearers (28.2%) reported driving more than two hours per day on average as opposed to only 14.9% of wearers.

Since a large proportion of the trips were work-related and travel to downtown from suburban areas involved driving on both highways and city streets, it was not surprising to find many drivers who reported such a combination as a representation of their normal trip pattern. A higher percentage of observed non-wearers than wearers placed their trips in this category (25.4% vs. 11.3%, respectively) and thus there may be more equivalence between city interviewees and highway subjects than might otherwise have been the case.

In spite of the fact that safety belt use was observed, it was felt that asking drivers about their use would be valuable. As has been discussed before, when it comes to safety belt wearing there is no such thing as always or never.

To prove this point, a little over 11% of all those interviewed stated that they did not consider themselves regular safety belt wearers even though almost 30% of them were observed to be not wearing at the time of the survey. Of the self-defined non-wearers, however, 82% were also observed to be not wearing.

For those who did consider themselves regular belt wearers, two-thirds said that there were no times when they did not wear. Not surprisingly, a higher proportion of observed wearers (73.0%) than non-wearers (42.9%) indicated that they always wore belts, but what is surprising is the latter percentage. Even though they had not worn their belts for two days in a row (i.e., morning work trips) or else on a high-speed highway, a substantial number of drivers were prepared to state that there were no conditions under which they would travel unrestrained!

A further **34.7%** of the observed non-wearers who claimed regular use habits admitted that they would likely not wear belts on short trips. This compares with only **16.6%** of observed, regular wearers.

In the group of those not considering themselves to be regular wearers, only two (less than 8%) admitted to never wearing and these were both observed non-wearers. For self-described non-regular wearers, the most popular reason for occasional wearing was when they suspected police checks (30%). All of these drivers were observed non-wearers. Other major reasons given for occasional use were when traveling on high-speed highways (22%) and when being a passenger in someone else's car (26%).

Finally, in the area of driving behavior, we asked our subjects if they considered themselves cautious drivers. Overall, an overwhelming 91% of them felt they were cautious and this was only slightly different between observed non-wearers (87%) and wearers (93%). Also, for the self-defined cautious drivers, the distributions of reasons given for their assessment were essentially identical for observed wearers and non-wearers. Good driving habits predominated in their self-descriptions. Unfortunately the small sample size of drivers who did not consider themselves as cautious precluded any meaningful analysis.

## Opinions about safety belts

Our beliefs about others' beliefs or feelings are an important measure of how we define what is real to us. Thus the drivers in our survey were asked how they think people generally feel towards safety belts. Two-thirds felt that people were in favor of them. Their responses displayed no significant differences between observed wearers and non-wearers with both responding most often (38%) that the majority of people probably think safety belts to be "a good idea."

When asked what they themselves felt, however, only 65% of the observed non-wearers responded in a similarly positive vein as compared to 86% of the observed wearers. Most of these positive responses again related simply to belts being "a good idea" but secondary feelings such as having "got used to them" and their being a safety requirement were also expressed. Again, observed non-wearers were underrepresented with respect to such responses (61% as opposed to 79% for wearers).

Of those drivers providing negative responses to the question about their own feelings toward restraints, the most often-given reason (45%) was that they "just didn't like them" or that they were uncomfortable or a nuisance. When these respondents were given an opportunity to explain their reasoning, the largest group (33%) felt that wearing should be a matter of personal choice and the second largest group (18%) cited discomfort. Observed non-wearers were significantly overrepresented in these two groups. The majority (56%) of those with positive feelings toward safety belt use expressed the conviction that restraints save lives and help prevent injuries.

Do drivers favor compulsory safety belt use laws? Predictably, a significantly higher proportion of our observed wearers than non-wearers did so (**86.9%** vs. **53.5%**, respectively). When asked why or why not, the majority (79%) of those in favor cited reasons dealing with safety and security. This was true of both observed wearers and non-wearers alike. For those not in favor of compulsory wearing, most (75%) gave "individual rights" as their reason for opposing it. This position was slightly overrepresented for non-wearers at 79% as compared to 71% for wearers.

A consideration that goes arm-in-arm with legislation is the perceived risk of apprehension. Overwhelmingly, our respondents felt the chances were either moderately or extremely low (76%). Observed wearers and non-wearers were in very close agreement with respect to this assessment.

In spite of the uniformly low rating of apprehension risk, about half (51%) of the drivers believed that fines should be successful in causing people to buckle up. Only about one-quarter of respondents felt fines were ineffective and a further 13% thought fines might work for some people but not for others. A somewhat smaller proportion of observed non-wearers (42%) than wearers (54%) had confidence in the efficacy of fines.

In explaining the reasons behind their positions, the largest group (67%) of those thinking fines to be effective cited people's dislike of having to part with "hard earned cash," especially if the fine were high enough to make it difficult to afford. This response was somewhat underrepresented in non-wearers at 57% as opposed to 70% for wearers.

For those not convinced of the usefulness of fines, the largest group (41%) were those who felt that such sanctions would not change behavior because of people's strong personal feelings. Next, at 30%, were those who cited people's insistence on freedom of choice as limiting the fines' effectiveness. This latter position was taken significantly more often with observed non-wearers (**47.8%**) than wearers (**18.4%**).

In light of the above results, it is not surprising that the majority of respondents considered fines to be a necessary form of control for restraint use. Of those who were observed not wearing, however, only 49% felt non-users should be fined as compared to 66% of those who were observed wearing. Interestingly, when asked how large the fines should be, the majority (51%) of those who favored fines thought they should be $25 or less. In other words, less than the currently applied level in British Columbia. Since this response was more popular with observed non-wearers (66%) than wearers (47%) it may be that some drivers wish to appear "on-side" with what they perceive as the majority-supported position (e.g., fines for non-use). At the same time they may not wish to be penalized unduly for breaking what they may still view as an optional code of conduct.

How drivers view others in relation to, or as a result of, these others' position on safety belt use is thus of some interest. We might expect that usual wearers would have a different outlook than usual non-wearers.

Only **17.3%** of our observed wearers expressed any positive feelings towards those who never wear safety belts. Not surprisingly, on the other hand, **42.3%** of the observed non-wearers had positive things to say about such people. The largest group of those who felt negatively towards full-time non-wearers was made up of those who were of the opinion that such people are irresponsible, careless or risk-takers. The contribution of observed wearers and non-wearers to this group was roughly proportional.

A somewhat larger proportion of observed non-wearers (15%) than wearers (8%) expressed less-than-positive feelings towards those people who always use restraints. Generally speaking, however, the vast majority of both observed wearers (92%) and observed non-wearers (85%) had reasonably good things to say about habitual belt wearers. Even in the case of the latter group, the majority viewed these people as smart, sensible or careful persons who value their lives. A slightly greater proportion of observed non-wearers than wearers even said they respected and/or supported such people! Evidently, most non-wearers have no desire to proselytize and seem content to accept the positions of others even if they cannot identify with them personally. This would certainly be consistent with the "freedom of choice" philosophy, which many non-wearers espouse.

## Views on other accident countermeasures

Returning to the validity-of-fines theme, we asked our interviewees what they thought about motorcyclists who rode unhelmeted and who had to pay a fine when caught. The great majority of respondents (70%) agreed that they should be penalized. Only a slightly smaller proportion of observed non-wearers (66%) than wearers (71%) answered in the affirmative.

Should all cars have a centre, high-mounted brakelight? When we asked this question of our surveyed drivers only 38% responded with an unequivocal yes. Almost as many (33%) gave a flat no, and the rest were either unsure or else felt that the benefits of such devices depended upon circumstance. There were no significant or even noticeable differences between observed wearers and non-wearers on this subject.

Reasons given in support of high-mounted brakelight use predominantly related to increased conspicuity and accident prevention. For those against the idea, main themes involved the notion of distraction for following drivers and the belief that these devices were simply not effective in reducing accidents. New cars were considered "fair game" for some but the added expense of universal retrofit was not.

One item of observation applied to drivers as they entered the parking lots was whether or not they had their headlights on (all observations were at normal daytime light levels). The use of daytime running lights has been promoted to the general public by safety councils and automobile associations as a prudent safety measure and it is still, at the time of writing, an entirely optional action. We might, therefore, anticipate that such "lights-on" activity would appeal to safety-conscious people.

While only 13% of drivers entering our interview sites had their headlights on, the percentage was much greater for the observed wearers than for the non-wearers (**16.5%** vs. **3.7%**, respectively). This certainly confirms the above hypothesis, but when we asked the subjects directly whether or not they always drove with headlights on in the daytime—fully 22% said yes (27% of observed wearers and 10% of non-wearers). Obviously, as with safety belt wearing, definitions of "always" do not necessarily equate with the reality of "always."

Reasons given for regular use of daytime headlights centred on improved conspicuity. Those who did not regularly use headlights during the day most often expressed the belief that they were useful only in poor visibility conditions or on highways. Predictably, a substantial proportion (18%) were against the idea because of the risk of a dead battery if one forgot to turn the lights off when parking. There were no measurable differences between the response patterns of observed wearers and non-wearers.

## Feelings about the police

The activities of traffic police are things about which many drivers have strong feelings—especially if they have ever been ticketed. We asked our interviewees how they felt most people viewed traffic police and then how they felt about them themselves.

Overall, only 34% of the drivers made positive statements about the public's perceived opinion of police. Of interest, though, was the fact that a slightly higher percentage (37%) of non-wearers than wearers (32%) had something positive to say. Of the negative responses, most common was the position that people just do not like them, resent them or have a low opinion of them (43%). The next most common theme was that people find traffic police a nuisance and annoying to have around, and this was followed by the belief that many people feel intimidated (made nervous) by them.

There were no evident differences in responses between observed wearers and non-wearers except for the positive notion that the police are "necessary for protection." A significantly higher proportion of observed non-wearer positive responses were in this category than was the case for observed wearers.

In contrast to the largely negative way our interviewees believed the motoring public felt about the police, they themselves apparently felt more positive. Over half (59%) gave favorable responses but the proportion for observed non-wearers was somewhat less, at 47%, than that for wearers (64%). There is a suggestion in this that non-wearers may have less positive attitudes toward police (perhaps resulting, in some cases, from being caught in safety belt checks) than do wearers. Again, a higher proportion of observed non-wearer responses were in the category of "necessary for protection" (69.7%) than was the case for observed wearers (37.0%).

Of those who didn't like traffic police, assessments of them as ineffective, annoying or arrogant were reported more frequently by observed non-wearers (46.4%) than by wearers (23.5%).

When given the opportunity to expand on their initial reactions, those responding positively (57%) tended to stress the good work police do in enforcing the law. There were no evident differences between observed wearers and non-wearers in this regard. In the case of those making negative comments, many (19%) felt that police should be targeting some group of drivers other than the one to which they (the respondents) belonged or else that police are simply trying to fill ticket quotas (18%). Again, no differences between observed wearer and non-wearer responses were observed.

## Attitudes toward traffic safety advertisements

The whole question of whether or not ads are effective in modifying behavior is subject to considerable controversy. This is not an area replete with unequivocal research findings. Nevertheless, over 70% of our interviewed drivers were convinced that current anti-drinking-driving media messages (public service announcements) were indeed effective in reducing the incidence of driving while impaired. In this, the observed non-wearers were slightly more certain than the wearers (78% vs. 68%, respectively).

When those who felt ads to be effective were asked why they thought so, the largest group of responses (52%) centred on the belief that such ads enhance awareness of the problem. Presumably awareness was assumed to lead directly to behavior change. Promotion of fear of apprehension was the next most commonly expounded reason that was given by 17% of the respondents. A somewhat smaller proportion of observed non-wearers cited fear as a reason why ads work (11% of those non-wearers who responded positively as compared to 20% for positively responding wearers).

Reasonings employed by those who felt that current ads were not effective were lead by the belief that ads would not influence the small group of troublemakers who will do what they want regardless (48%). There was also a feeling that ads are not tough enough and are ineffective when compared to police enforcement (28%). In neither of these two main response areas was there any differences between observed wearers and non-wearers.

When the drivers were asked what kind of ads they thought would be most effective in reducing impaired driving, the bulk of responses were fairly evenly divided amongst a few main categories. Over 21%, for example, wanted "blood and guts" accident scenes. Somewhat related to this shock approach was another popular suggestion that ads should stress subsequent accident consequences (e.g., suffering victims and grieving friends or relatives). The other large group of respondents (20%) voted to retain the status quo. They were in favor of continuing whatever is being done now. In all of this, there were no apparent differences between observed wearers and non-wearers.

## Driver record contents

The great majority of drivers (88%) had no accidents during the preceding two-year period. Even going back five years before the interviews, only 23% had been involved in one or more reported accidents. In both the two- and five-year periods, the observed non-wearers had a higher proportion of drivers with one or more accidents (14% at 2 years and 29% at 5 years) than did wearers (11% at 2 years and 21% at 5 years) but these differences were not great enough to be judged significant.

In terms of traffic law violations, **48.3%** of observed non-wearers had at least one conviction within the last two years as against **31.5%** for wearers. The difference between the two groups increased in significance when we went back over a five-year period. In this period, we found that 72% of the observed non-wearers had one or more convictions compared to 52% for the observed wearers.

An examination of conviction types yielded few important discoveries. It appeared that the greater proportion of convictions for observed non-wearing drivers was due largely to an excess of major operational violations (such as disobeying license restrictions and failure to wear a safety belt) and, to a much lesser extent, major social behavior violations (predominantly drinking-driving). Predictably, the group of observed non-wearers had a greater proportion of drivers with one or more previous convictions for safety belt non-use (**18.3%**) than did the observed wearers (**6.2%**).

Of course, any comparison of accumulated accidents and convictions can be substantially affected by other variables and especially those describing driving experience and exposure. Even other apparent differences between the observed safety belt wearers and non-wearers may be due to the influence of other factors apart from restraint use. This is why multivariate forms of analysis are commonly employed as will be described in the following section.

# Multivariate Analysis of the Survey Data

Chapter 9 introduced the concept of multivariate analysis—specifically in terms of multiple regression. Here we will examine a somewhat different process but the concept remains the same.

Many of the attitudinal responses in the questionnaire were, being complex, open-ended and expressions of opinion, not amenable to a multivariate approach. The demographic-driving exposure responses together with the observational and driver record data were, however, suitable for such treatment. These data included driver age, income level, marital status, gender, driving experience, location of most driving, model year of vehicle, observed safety belt use, average annual rate of past accidents, and average annual rate of past violation convictions. The latter two variables were based on a five-year record prior to the date of the survey (less than four percent of the interviewed drivers reported having been driving for less than five years) and normalized using a square-root transformation. Since driver age and length of driving experience were very highly associated (a 91% degree of correlation) and since age was controlled for in sample selection, only "experience," of these two variables, was utilized in the analysis. In any event, the "young driver factor" was not in evidence since the youngest age present was 20.

In addition to the socio-demographic variables described above, data were also collected on self-reported wearing under different driving situations. A variable representing the subjects' inclination to change their regular wearing habits under a variety of conditions was created. Six different conditions were identified dealing with such things as length of trip, role as driver or passenger, presumed hazard level of driving conditions, presence or absence of law enforcement, and influence of family or friends. The final category for the variable was for those who said they would maintain their use or non-use under all conditions.

One main purpose in pursuing this multivariate investigation was to find out whether the apparent differences in accident and conviction rates between observed wearers and non-wearers were real. That is, whether or not they were simply the product of other relationships in the data and not a function of driver characteristics related to belt wearing at all. Another purpose was to compare the effects of socio-demographic variables and situational variables in predicting observed wearing behavior.

In order to meet these objectives, we performed a discriminant analysis using observed belt wearing (yes or no) as the categorical variable. In other words, we asked what characteristics significantly and independently distinguished the observed wearers from the observed non-wearers.

Two hundred and thirty-six complete records were available for this analysis with 71 (30%) being observed non-wearers. With accident and conviction record data included, the total was reduced to 164 (again, 30% being observed non-wearers). Only two of the above listed socio-demographic variables proved significant in the smaller sample: daytime headlight use, and number of recorded convictions. When compared with observed safety belt wearers, the observed non-wearers were significantly less likely to be driving with their headlights on (in daytime) and had significantly higher annual conviction rates for driving infractions.

At best, however, such a description could only correctly categorize less than 60% of the drivers. The concept of a "typical" wearer, and a "typical" non-wearer may thus not be very useful in practice.

When the situational variable was included in the analysis, the last category (i.e., no situations under which wearing behavior would change) was highly significant (at better than 99% confidence) and, in fact, totally replaced the violation record and daytime headlight use variables in the results. In addition, the vehicle model year was significant at the 95% confidence level. The influence of driving situation was in the direction of greater belt wearing consistency for observed wearers. Observed non-wearers were significantly more likely to report changing their regular behavior under a range of driving situations than were the observed wearers (**64.6%** vs. **25.0%**, respectively). When compared with observed wearers, the non-wearers were also more likely to be driving older vehicles (especially cars more than 10 years old).

As outlined at the beginning of this chapter, the original observed samples were selected to approximately match wearers and non-wearers by age and gender. Thus it is not surprising that the generally accepted finding of lower wearing rates by young (or inexperienced) males (e.g., Wagenaar et al., 1987) was not in evidence. Our survey results may confirm Wagenaar's (1987) finding of lower socioeconomic status associated with safety belt non-wearers as evidenced, in our case, by association with older (but still safety-belt equipped) vehicles.

Using the full interview sample (with driver record information removed from the analysis) and with the situational behavior variable included, 70% of the drivers were correctly grouped through consideration of just two highly significant (at the 99% level) variable categories: the overall inclination towards inconsistent belt wearing behavior in different situations (which was a characteristic of observed non-wearers), and the specific tendency to wear or not wear depending on the perceived likelihood of apprehension or sanctions. This latter factor also characterized observed non-wearer behavior.

Vehicle age and use of headlights were also identified as discriminators at a lower (95%) level of significance.

The main conclusions arising out of the analyses were: (1) the observed safety belt non-wearers had accumulated a significantly higher level of convictions than had the wearers (the same could not be said for accidents when all other variable effects were taken into account); and (2) the observed non-wearers were more likely than the wearers to report modifying their usual belt use (or non-use) behavior in different situations. This latter finding contradicts Wagenaar's conclusions.

# Knowledge Gained in the Conduct of a Large-Scale Safety Belt Wearing Survey

As part of the major 1987 safety belt wearing campaign detailed in chapter 11, pre- and post-campaign surveys were conducted in which drivers were interviewed about their belt wearing (or non-wearing). Some observational data were also obtained.

The analysis which follows is based on amalgamation of pre and post samples. The total sample size of observed and interviewed drivers is thus over 9,000. As in the discussion of results from the smaller—but more intensive—interview survey reported previously, significant differences in sample subset proportions will be indicated by placing the comparisons in bold type.

# Why do wearers wear and non-wearers not?

Four groups of drivers were identified based on observed wearing behavior and responses to questions concerning use of belts: (1) drivers wearing belts who said they always wore them; (2) drivers wearing belts who admitted to occasional non-wearing; (3) drivers not belted who stated that they never or hardly ever wore them; and (4) drivers not belted who said there were times when they did use restraints.

The major difference in behavior justification between groups 1 and 2 was related to safety. Wearers who said they always wore belts cited safety as the overwhelming primary reason (**54.6%**). Previous accidents, while not common, were nevertheless alluded to by between two and three percent of respondents. Observed but admitted part-time wearers, on the other hand, were significantly less convinced by the safety argument since they identified with this reason only **27.6%** of the time. Other than safety and the law, this latter group mentioned a wide variety of difficult-to-categorize responses.

Drivers observed unrestrained and who stated that they almost never wore safety belts cited discomfort as the predominant reason for their decision (**44.8%**). Next to this, the largest single group of responses dealt with freedom of choice (10%). By comparison, unbelted drivers who described themselves as occasional wearers were almost totally unconcerned with any possible safety belt discomfort and the level of response in this category was significantly below that for full-time non-wearers (**5.3%**). Reasons for not wearing by this latter group tended to be framed as excuses for a momentary lapse; they simply forgot (22%) or they were only on a short trip (47%).

## Are day and time important factors in observed wearing behavior?

The results of the survey showed no significant differences in safety belt wearing rate by day of week nor by time of day. It should be noted that evening survey periods did not extend into late night or early morning when drinking drivers were likely to be about nor were the survey locations selected in such a way as to make encountering such persons likely in any event.

## Do roadway conditions and trip characteristics play a role?

Given the probable increased perception of danger associated with precipitation and wet roads, it might be supposed that more drivers would buckle up under such conditions. In fact, slightly more did (80% vs. 79% under dry conditions), but the difference was not enough to be significant.

On the other hand, traveling on highways as opposed to city streets had a substantial impact on belt-wearing behavior. When the observed and interviewed drivers were asked to describe their current trip in terms of the extent of highway involvement, a significantly greater percent of restrained than unrestrained drivers said that their trips involved some highway travel (**21.6%** vs. **11.9%**, respectively).

Similar differences were also reflected in terms of trip length. A significantly greater percentage of non-wearers were engaged in short trips (< 2 km) than was the case for wearers (**58.4%** vs. **38.6%**, respectively). Alternately, a significantly greater percent of wearers (**17.4%**) than non-wearers (**8.1%**) were on trips longer than 10 km.

## Driver demographics and experience as factors in restraint use

A significantly higher proportion of female drivers (**83.1%**) than male drivers (**73.6%**) were observed to be wearing safety belts.

Safety belt wearing was relatively high for very young drivers (16 and 17 years old) but decreased markedly for those ages 18 to 21. Thereafter, the wearing percentage increased steadily. The trend is shown in figure 8 and, while few adjacent percentages are significantly different, the overall picture is reasonably clear. It also confirms the relationship between age and belt wearing for those ages 16 to 21 reported in our publication *Rethinking Young Drivers* (Rothe, 1987).

**Figure 8**
**Observed Safety Belt Wearing by Drivers of Different Ages**

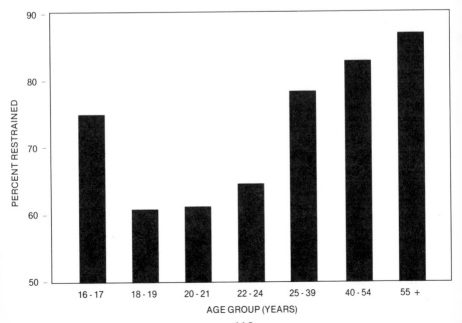

Similar results were found when comparing restraint use with reported driving experience. Those with one-year experience or less were belted 81% of the time whereas the wearing rate for those with two to three-years' experience dropped to 70%—a large decrease but not significant due to the relatively small sample sizes involved in these experience categories. The trend of belt wearing by experience level is shown in figure 9. Only the difference between 6 to 15 years, and 16 to 40 years is significant in all the adjacent cell comparisons but the shape of the distribution is very similar with respect to age.

**Figure 9**
**Observed Safety Belt Wearing as a Function of Driving Experience**

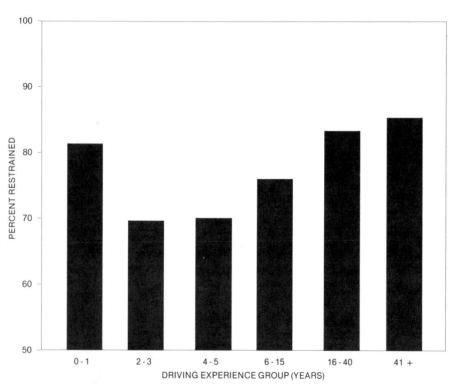

Looking at the relationships another way, however, we find that the non-wearers had a significantly higher proportion of drivers with less than six years' driving experience (**16.5%** vs. **10.6%**) and a significantly higher proportion of drivers under 22 years of age (**16.0%** vs. **8.3%**) than those observed wearing safety belts. Since the minimum driving age in British Columbia is 16, these two results express essentially the same phenomenon.

### Are wearing differences associated with attitudinal differences?

One of the first attitudinal factors encountered during the survey was expressed by agreement or refusal to be interviewed. While only **4.0%** of those wearing safety belts declined to be interviewed, **9.0%** of non-wearers refused to talk to the survey personnel.

Attitude towards safety was addressed through questions related to behavior in using headlights during the daytime and having installed a special high-mounted brakelight (for those with vehicles not having such a factory-equipped brakelight).

Significantly more wearers than non-wearers reported using daytime headlights (**74.0%** vs. **63.3%**, respectively), although there were no differences between the two groups in the frequency of different circumstances reported under which daytime headlights would be used. In terms of brakelights, **8.3%** of belted drivers in non-factory-equipped vehicles had installed the new high-mounted devices while only **4.4%** of unbelted drivers in such vehicles had done so.

# Wearers and Non-Wearers in the Accident Database

Another means at our disposal for exploring differences between safety belt wearers and non-wearers was to use an accident-involved driver database consisting of matched police files, Motor Vehicle Department data, and insurance records. As described in the Appendices, a sample consisting of 500 non-wearers (reported as unrestrained at the time of the accident in a vehicle equipped with belts and, additionally, having at least one previous conviction for non-wearing) and 500 wearers (reported as buckled-up in the crash and also having no previous safety belt charges or convictions) was established. The restrictive definition of non-wearers determined the size of this subset and the similarly-sized subset of wearers was then selected from the many thousands of such records in a representative manner based on fifteen different driver demographic and accident locational variables.

The variables available with our sample of 1,000 accident-involved drivers included the circumstances surrounding the crash (e.g., ambient conditions, driver actions, etc.); the police-assigned factors contributing to the accident together with charges laid (if any); and the past driving records of the vehicle operators and driver demographic variables such as age, gender, experience and average income level of dwelling area.

Past accidents and convictions were expressed as averages per year of driving experience up to a maximum of seven years, and then normalized using a square-root transformation.

A discriminant analysis was undertaken using belt wearing as the group or classification variable. Seventy-seven percent of the belt-wearing cases and 66% of the non-wearing cases were correctly grouped based on seven variables. The factors that significantly discriminated between wearers and non-wearers at the 99% confidence level were as follows:

1. **Accident contributing factors related to driver condition**
   Safety belt non-wearers had six times the incidence of such police-assigned factors (mainly related to alcohol involvement) as did wearers (**24.0%** vs. **4.3%**, respectively); without this factor as an independent variable in the analysis, the variable representing the presence of past drinking-driving convictions came out as significant.

2. **Gender**
   Safety belt non-wearers were more likely to be male than were the wearers (**86.4%** vs. **66.5%**, respectively).

3. **Number of convictions (other than for safety belt non-use) per year of driving experience**
   Safety belt non-wearers had twice the level of past recorded convictions than the wearers did (**1.64** vs. **0.84**, respectively). (Accidents were highly related to convictions and not independently significant, but non-wearers had **0.25** per year vs. only **0.18** for wearers.)

4. **Type of vehicle driven**
   Safety belt non-wearers were more likely to be driving trucks and less likely to be driving passenger cars than wearers (**64.2%** vs. **81.3%**, respectively for cars).

5. **Age**
   Safety belt non-wearers were more likely to belong to the young age groups than were the wearers, especially the 19-25 age group where the proportions were **41.9%** and **25.8%**, respectively.

As noted previously, in the analysis both accident and conviction rates were transformed by taking the square root so as to more closely approximate a normal (symmetrical) distribution. Many drivers had no past accidents and few violations. The values reported above, however, are the actual and not the normalized ones. One further variable fell short of significance at the 99% confidence level but was significant at better than 95% confidence:

6. **Average dwelling unit annual income**
   Safety belt non-wearers lived in communities having lower average dwelling unit income than was the case for wearers (**$16,877** vs. **$17,356**, respectively).

In addition to the above-mentioned factors, there were several other areas of comparison which were significantly different on a univariate basis. For example, safety belt non-wearers were more likely to be assigned accident contributing factors by police and also more likely to be judged responsible for the crash.

Such a finding confirms the accident fault differential proposed at the beginning of this chapter. As mentioned previously, the presence of past convictions for drinking-driving offences was important, with non-wearers significantly overrepresented in this category. Consistent with this was the fact that the non-wearers had five times the level of involvement during the midnight-to-three a.m. time period that the wearers did (**18.3%** vs. **3.9%** respectively).

Another factor proving to be significantly different on a univariate basis was one which is closely tied to the late-night time period. A greater proportion of non-wearer accidents happened on Saturdays than was the case for wearers. Seemingly related to this late-night weekend scenario was the greater proportion of highway crashes attributed to non-wearers than wearers.

Finally, our earlier findings in the young drivers study (Rothe, 1987) with respect to passengers were confirmed. Safety belt non-wearing drivers carried a greater average number of passengers (**0.69** per vehicle) than did wearers (**0.55** per vehicle).

# Driver-Passenger Relationships in the Data

As illustrated in chapter 6, our consideration of driver-passenger influences is based on the philosophical construct that we define ourselves through other people. How other people relate to us influences our behavior. As well, it influences their behavior towards us.

The influence of other people on our behavior in different situations has been emphasized in numerous sociological and social-psychological studies (Lewin, 1951). In brief, these studies indicated that social factors in different situations confront actors with conflicts, pressures and opportunities. These influence the actor's actions and views.

In life, each person experiences numerous relationships. For the purpose of clarity, but not necessarily exclusivity, we can define these as imposed structural relationships and negotiated structural relationships. Examples of imposed structural relationships are members of a family, students in a classroom, members of a church congregation, or colleagues at work. Individuals' relationships with others in an ordered group setting are controlled, or imposed upon, by rules of conduct that are enforced by tradition, formal policy, legal creed, or institutional expectations.

Negotiated structural relationships are between group members who are tied by taken-for-granted rules but whose interactions can be negotiated according to the situations. For example, sport clubs are structured. But the extent to which members interrelate is not based so much on an imposed meaning as it is based on negotiated interests, images, and so on, among members whose driving context may relate to drinking, partying or dating. The relationships are sustained as long as members' images are not damaged or feelings of belonging are not jeopardized.

Our involvement in so many groups is referred to by Simmel (1955) as the "web of group affiliations." We interrelate differently with people next to us based on whether our relationship is built on a negotiated or imposed structure. Because the web is so intricate, it is almost impossible to pinpoint one major group-related influence. We must, therefore, generalize on the basis of greatest probability. Age-related group affiliations have normally been applied to make sense of young peoples' peer relationships and young peoples' family ties. This becomes a workable approach for looking at young driver-passenger relationships and safety belt wearing.

Of the 1,000 drivers in our accident sample, 181 were carrying passengers. In order to investigate further the influence of passengers on driver safety belt use, we obtained in each case the belt wearing, age and gender of the passenger seated closest to the driver. We then defined four possible passenger-rider "relationships" by age:

1. **Peer**
   A passenger whose age was within seven years of the driver's ($\pm$ 6 years maximum); the minimum age for drivers' peers was assumed to be 14 (the average age in first-year high school).
2. **Parent**
   A passenger 20 years or more older than the driver.
3. **Older colleague/relative**
   A passenger between seven and 20 years older than the driver.
4. **Younger friend/relative**
   A passenger seven years or more younger than the driver.

Using the above age-related definitions, we looked at the effect that passenger presence appeared to have on the belt wearing behavior of young drivers (under age 30). In the comparisons presented, it should be borne in mind that calculated wearing rates are generally lower than would be expected for the British Columbia driving population owing to the sampling design which balanced the number of wearers and non-wearers.

Imposed structural relationships would more likely be expected to exist between young drivers (of either gender) and parents or older colleagues and relatives. Negotiated structural relationships, on the other hand, would more likely be exemplified by peer-group associations. Because of the officially unsanctioned nature of safety belt non-use, we might expect that young drivers carrying passengers with whom they are involved in an imposed structural relationship (i.e., parents and older colleagues/relatives) would be more likely belted than those carrying passengers with whom such structural relationships are negotiated (i.e., peers).

In our accident-involved driver sample, the safety belt wearing rate for young drivers having a peer-group passenger was **35.5%**. However, when the passenger was, according to our definitions, an older colleague, relative or parent, the average wearing rate was much higher at **63.2%** (**77.8%** and **58.6%** for parents and older colleagues, respectively). This difference was highly significant statistically.

Driver safety belt wearing was apparently also related to the wearing behavior of the passenger. For example, young drivers transporting parents or older colleagues/relatives who were belted had a wearing rate of 86%. Even young male drivers were found to have a relatively high wearing rate (71%) when with belted young male passengers. Such a result would suggest either that safety belt wearing behavior is negotiated within a particular situation or else that persons of similar dispositions tend to associate in the first place.

Both postulates could be applicable, but we found evidence to support the situational or contextual effect in the difference between dating-age (16 to 25 year old) male and female passenger behavior. The young males of this age group in our sample were only 1.3 times more likely to be unrestrained when traveling as a passenger of an unbelted young male driver than they were when driving themselves. Young females, however, were 2.4 times more likely not to wear their safety belts when with an unbelted young male driver than they were as drivers themselves. The fact that young females are considerably more likely, on their own, to be belt wearers than young males, means that inevitably they may find themselves in a dating situation with a young man (as driver) who does not wear a safety belt. In such a situation, the above results seem to indicate clearly that young females often modify their normal restraint use behavior to conform to that of their male companion. The situation described by the young female as previously reported in chapter 6 is thus probably not an uncommon one.

> I usually didn't wear one (safety belt) when I was first going out with my present boyfriend. I felt that if I buckled up and sat on the far side of the car he might see me as being cold and distant. It was a relationship I wanted to continue so I sat over by him.

Similarly, for young male drivers the influence exerted by peer-group passengers was seemingly different depending on whether the latter were male or female. While such drivers had wearing rates of 37% and 38% when traveling alone or with female peers, respectively, their belt use when accompanied by male peers was only 26%. With the relatively small sample sizes involved, the difference was not quite significant but the direction of the effect supports the notion of negotiated safety belt wearing behavior within peer-group relationships.

It is reasonable to conclude from the foregoing discussion that safety belt wearing by vehicle occupants is likely to be influenced by companions—whether drivers or passengers. The structural relationship between vehicle occupants—whether imposed or negotiated—is important in influencing restraint use. Wearing of a safety belt, especially for young people, depends on the nature of the social situation with respect to in-car companions and thus may vary from one context to another.

# Demographics, Situation and Context

In our discussion of safety belt wearing behavior in this chapter, we have given most weight to the observational study of 380 drivers and the analysis of 1,000 accident-involved drivers. Our statistical comparisons identified several important socio-demographic variables such as age and gender; socioeconomic variables such as average income in area of residence and type and age of vehicle driven; general behavioral variables such as the accumulation of prior accidents and convictions; and situationally-related variables such as drinking-driving, nighttime driving and wearing consistency under different conditions.

It is inevitable that these results will be compared with the recent findings in the Michigan study (Wagenaar et al., 1987) where the investigators concluded that situational variables were less important than socio-demographic ones in explaining individual safety belt wearing behavior. There were, however, important differences between these two observational studies, and also undoubtedly differences between the non-wearing population of British Columbia and Michigan.

For example, the Michigan study was conducted among an observed non-wearing population consisting of over 50% of the state's drivers, and interviewees were selected based on a single observation of belt use. Further, drivers were contacted in such a way and the survey instrument was presented in such a format that they would likely have been aware of both the observational record and the objectives of the questioning.

By comparison, our study, while considerably smaller in scope, was designed to include repeat observations and to ensure that the observation and the purpose of the survey were not obvious to the drivers being interviewed. People may respond differently to questions about an illegal behavior when they know they have been observed "in the act" than if they are unaware that the questioner knows something about their actions.

In addition, we were dealing with a more "condensed" observed non-wearer population which constituted only about 20% of all drivers. Both British Columbia and Michigan have a safety belt wearing law but British Columbia's has been in effect for a much longer period. British Columbia drivers who do not regularly buckle up have therefore had time to develop and rationalize all kinds of non-wearing situations or contexts, which can coexist with a system of official disapproval of non-wearing behavior (see chapter 5). As safety belt wearing rates increase in U.S. states, it may be found that situational variables assume an increasingly important role in predicting which drivers (and passengers) will or will not be restrained at any given time.

It is also possible to interpret certain variables, which Wagenaar et al. classed as socio-demographic, in a situational context. For example, the authors of the Michigan study identified drivers in urban environments as one of the socio-demographic groups which should be targeted for belt use programs. This group may, of course, be reflecting a situational use pattern as well as a socio-demographic pattern. In addition, the authors characterized drinking to intoxication as a significant socio-demographic variable in that non-users were more likely to report such activity. This can also be viewed from a situational perspective since we know from roadside alcohol surveys that drivers who have been drinking are less likely to be buckled up.

But even if most of the Michigan drivers did indeed not "selectively use belts in certain situations and not in others" (Wagenaar et al., 1987), such a conclusion does not address the contextual issue raised in chapters 5 and 6. The situations defined in the Michigan study were broad ones dealing with such things as trip origin, destination and purpose. Certainly, peoples' wearing behavior may be generally consistent whether they are going shopping or driving to work but in either of these situations, belts may or may not be worn in a given instance or at a certain juncture within the trip duration. Such behavior relates not so much to the overall purpose of trips or the general, broad social situation in which vehicle occupants find themselves, but rather to specific events which arise within the context of the trip. For example, friends traveling together may generally observe belt-wearing rules but in the context of a heated discussion, or with the need to retrieve an object from behind the back seat, or in the act of eating and drinking, they may temporarily suspend their normal wearing behavior.

Demographic variables are indeed important indicators of likely wearing behavior. Males, and especially young males, are more frequently observed to be unrestrained than are other drivers. But even for this group, it is our contention that wearing or non-wearing often has a contextual aspect. Moreover, understanding such contextual behavior holds considerably more potential for promoting long-term change regardless of the demographic groups targeted, than does a simple identification of these "high-risk" categories.

# How Practical is Significance? Some Final Thoughts

Before we leave the subject of differences in attitudinal and behavioral characteristics between safety belt wearers and non-wearers, there is an important point worth considering. Even though there were significant differences between average values of these characteristics as representative of groups defined as wearers and non-wearers (by observation or from accident data), there were also substantial variances associated with the means.

The mean, or average, of a set of values is referred to as a measure of "central tendency." As such, differences between means may be tested within the context of their associated variations and found to be significantly different in a statistical sense. But the mean is a contrived figure, so to speak. No actual such driver may exist and, furthermore, even when the means of two groups of drivers are significantly different, many drivers in one group will be indistinguishable from those in the other, and vice versa.

In the accident sample, the non-wearers were not as efficiently discriminated (66% correctly classified) as were the wearers (77% correctly classified). In both accident and interview samples, the non-wearing group was thus characterized by inconsistency.

The foregoing analyses allow us to conclude that certain demographic and driving characteristics are more common among probable non-wearers than probable wearers, but they do not provide a reliable profile of a non-wearer toward which countermeasures can efficiently or uniformly be directed. Using all the significant characteristics together could be somewhat impractical and likely unsuccessful, while using only a few would be inefficient. Wagenaar et al. (1987), while recommending the use of socio-demographic variables in defining audiences for safety belt messages, recognized that: "if these variables alone are used to target policies and programs to increase safety belt use, a substantial proportion of the non-users in the state will not be targeted and many safety belt users will unintentionally be targeted for special efforts."

Take the category, gender, for example. While defined accident-involved non-wearers were indeed more likely to be male than wearers, 14% of the former group were female and 34% of the latter group were male. If we directed safety belt propaganda towards only males, we would hit the wrong target almost 25% of the time. Similarly, while the average conviction history of non-wearers was significantly higher in both accident and survey samples than that for wearers, 10% and 39%, respectively of the former had only one conviction in five to seven years or no convictions at all. On the other hand, how likely are we to be able to identify, reach and influence all high-accident and high-conviction young males with low incomes who drive trucks?

Another problem is that not all the people we observed or defined as wearers or non-wearers at a particular time and place will necessarily maintain the same classification even throughout similar times and locations. Some will be on short trips, some will be on long trips; some will be with friends, others will be alone; and some will be involved in in-car activities or will be wearing their "best clothes," others will not. To an outside observer not privy to the individual wearing choices being continuously made, the presence of each driver in one group or the other might appear to be somewhat random. A number of drivers may be switching back and forth between wearing and non-wearing in such a way that a sort of "steady-state" condition exists over a given time period and on a province-wide or even on a local community basis. Thus a safety belt survey may be an accurate representation of this state, but the apparently repeatable results entirely mask the transient nature of the phenomenon. What is really happening is not uncovered by the survey.

Such a situation has a rough parallel in the air we breath. All the molecules are moving around randomly in all directions but successive snapshots taken under similar atmospheric conditions would show essentially the same number of molecules in the picture. If we had painted names or numbers on each molecule, however, we would see a markedly different arrangement.

While it may be useful for us to know what characteristics are most important in distinguishing regular or usual wearers from non-wearers, the fact remains that many people switch group membership for temporary reasons not covered by such general characteristics. Webb et al. (1988) also postulated such an explanation for the lack of consistency in adult belt wearing, which they observed under essentially identical repeat conditions. Such a situation makes it seem more reasonable to tailor education towards all drivers with emphasis on what we have called contextual behavior instead of, or in addition to, targeting certain demographic groups or those individuals who have specific, identifiable characteristics.

# CHAPTER 11

# SAFETY BELT
# WEARING MISSIONS

# Introduction

Safety belt wearing has, over the last ten years, entered an era of mobilization of consciousness. For reasons illustrated in this book, a significant group of motorists does not buckle up. Although the trend towards greater wearing is becoming evident, still for some organizations or institutions the number of people who wear safety belts is now growing too gradually. The growth of wearing rate constitutes a rapidly leveling climb beyond the 70% to 80% mark in British Columbia.

Groups all over North America have consciously and steadfastly defined the lack of safety belt wearing as a major societal problem. Public, private, and voluntary institutions have organized to help ameliorate the perceived problem. A quick glance at the list of governmental, charitable, and public health-sponsored agencies for traffic safety and occupant restraint usage in any North American metropolitan area confirms the growth of interest groups.

Over the years the groups have become more visible and dominant. For example, in the United States each state has a prestigious governor's traffic safety commission or a traffic safety office. At the local level we find examples of organizations such as the Minnesota Occupant Restraint Program, the Austin County Safety Belt Project, or the Lincoln Nebraska Seatbelt Safety Squad. In British Columbia, we have the Traffic Safety Education Department housed within the Insurance Corporation of British Columbia.

As a rule of thumb, none of the interested organizations consider the actual wearing to be anywhere near to what it should be. The ideal goal is, of course, 100 percent. In the United States, belt use remains below 50 percent in most research jurisdictions (Insurance Institute for Highway Safety, 1987). In British Columbia, according to the latest province-wide survey, the wearing rate is approximately 80 percent. The difference between measured reality and ideal differs from country to country and, in Canada, from province to province. Nevertheless, traffic safety organizations in all parts of North America strive towards their goal of total wearing. They are concerned with ends.

Nelson and Moffit (1988) believe that the reason there is such slow growth in safety belt wearing is because of program implementation, and theory and measurement failures. To compensate, some groups have stressed the implementation component. They select specific actions with broad community support to further their ideological positions. For an organization like the Insurance Corporation of British Columbia, maximum province-wide community support is solicited to promote the theme that people who do not buckle up are considered to be physical risks to themselves and other occupants in a vehicle, economic risks to society, and moral risks to members of society who believe in a code of responsibility. Safety belt non-wearers make conscious decisions, and their decisions are considered to be unsafe. As a consequence, it is believed, such motorists are likely to engage in other unsafe roadway behavior and to burden society with additional costs should they become involved in an accident. To make the highways safe, someone must take the responsibility. This becomes the mission.

# Missions for Health

It is nearly impossible to read a newspaper, to watch television, or to listen to the radio without being told what constitutes healthy living. Armed with epidemiological research findings and risk factor rationalizations, groups have sprung up almost everywhere in North America. For example, we are told that jogging and physical exercise, not smoking, adhering to low-fat diets, avoiding illicit drugs, participating only in safe sex, and regularly using safety belts lead to a healthier body and a better quality of life. By reducing our personal health risks, we have a greater chance to realize a truly good life.

To press their perspectives on a safer life, certain groups and organizations have designed rigorous intervention strategies. They lobby the federal, provincial and municipal governments with statistics, logic and emotion. In Canada, the non-smoking lobby has put pressure on the federal government to ban cigarette advertising including sponsorship of cultural and sports events, and to make federal installations like airports smoke-free. At the municipal level, some cities have been designated as smoke-free environments. Smoking in public buildings has been banned. Years of carefully planned media attention, countless presentations before elected officials, and many education campaigns have resulted in changes toward a healthier society. Organizations have used a strategy of cancer warnings to promote and facilitate this change.

Smoking is but one example of a health risk mission on the verge of success. In the past decade, people have become sensitized to the medical consequences of all kinds of social behavior. As Kitterie (1971) wrote, the move symbolizes the "coming of the therapeutic scale."

Many actions are understood through a host-agent-environment model. Behaviors are comprehended in terms of their causes and they can be prevented once the causal factors are known. Alcoholism is a social behavior which has undergone a redefinition from moral weakness to disease. Alcoholics are no longer arrested for public drunkenness. They are treated by organizations such as Alcoholics Anonymous or hospital clinics. The perspective on drinking has become part of the public health strategy.

# Safety Belt Wearing Proponents

Use or non-use of safety belts is socially influenced in some jurisdictions and legally controlled in others. Regardless of the baselines, safety belt usage is sanctioned, accepted, and expected to be accomplished by different groups.

An interpretation of Gusfield (1986) leads us to declare that within the groups' thinking, safety belt wearing has a moral connotation associated with a style of life—a patterned system of behavior regulating a wide range of actions. Safety belt wearing, it is argued, has special functions. For example, it symbolizes love for members of the family, responsibility for self, and general caring. It follows closely the moral slogan, "Have you hugged your child today?" Not wearing a belt and not encouraging children, friends, and family members to wear one are indications of irresponsible and poor moral adjustment.

To help resonate with the people, safety belt promotional groups spend considerable time, energy, and expertise. They would like citizens to understand the constituted nature of safety belt wearing and the moral-economic-legal-political forces. Rather than allowing buckling up to be a convenience, it must be turned to compulsion. "Get into the habit" is the preferred aphorism. If the personal moral approach lacks legitimacy with some people, a more objective tactic is offered. The moral-economic-legal-political line is crystallized as moral sentiment. For instance, a recently distributed document on restraint use and the law read:

> In one of the leading Canadian decisions dealing with seatbelt defence, Mr. Justice Monroe of the British Columbia Supreme Court reduced an award by 25 percent because of a plaintiff's negligence in failing to wear a seatbelt. Mr. Justice Monroe said, "a person must use reasonable care and take proper precautions for his own safety, and such precautions include the use of an available seatbelt (Yuan vs. Farstad, 1967)."

> . . . few cases involving failure to wear seatbelts ever come to court because of the general practice that most automobile accident claims are settled out of court. At the present time in Canada, where expert opinion indicates that failure to wear a seatbelt contributed to the injury, lawyers are becoming sufficiently sophisticated in this area to advise their clients of the offset that courts would likely

award. However, because of the significant effect that seatbelts have on preventing serious injuries and death, conviction under a statute for failure to wear a seatbelt could have a similar effect on a person's insurance premiums . . .

There is also the aspect of statutory standards governing the use of child restraint systems. With an increasing emphasis on the rights of children and their access to independent legal representation, where parents fail to take appropriate measures to ensure that their children are adequately placed in a seatbelt assembly, and these children suffer injuries directly caused by such failure, an action will lie against their parents for such negligence.

In Ohleiser vs. Cummings, Mr. Justice MacPherson stated as follows:

When we all pay for one another's hospital and medical care and other loss through taxes for insurance, we have a right to say to a driver and to a passenger: "Fasten your seatbelts in my interest if not in your own. If you don't fasten them then you may have to pay part of your loss if you are hurt." What we have here is not a new interference with private rights but the creation of a new public duty in the automobile age.

The courts have taken the authority to make morally binding announcements on the use of restraints. The legitimacy of moral force is now chained to economic repercussions which a driver faces when meeting a bad fate. What is situationally moral—the right thing for a father to do for his child—has turned to a question of what is societally moral based on insurance risk and social responsibility.

A recent issue of the Insurance Institute For Highway Safety "Status Report" provided evaluation results of two safety belt wearing campaigns organized by the National Highway Traffic Safety Administration. For successful missions, organizations are encouraged to adopt the following strategies:

1. Enforcement strategies should combine a blitz approach to be followed by continued enforcement during regular duties.
2. Public information and education must accompany an enforcement strategy.
3. A training program should be designed to create positive attitudes among police officers (IIHS, 1987).

In British Columbia, a leading campaign-oriented organization is the Insurance Corporation of British Columbia. Through the Traffic Safety Education Department, the Corporation serves to gather common and consensual views within institutions and organizations such as educational systems, municipal governments, provincial and municipal police detachments, public health facilities, businesses, industries and service clubs among others. Implementation strategies are designed on the basis of co-operation from these units.

# One Mission, Two Campaigns

The Insurance Corporation of British Columbia spends considerable time and money to increase compliance with safety belt legislation on an ongoing basis, and at selected junctures it has promoted major province-wide campaigns. The first noteworthy campaign occurred in 1983 and the second one took place in 1987.

## The First Campaign

In the summer of 1983, the Insurance Corporation of British Columbia initiated a safety belt wearing promotion entitled, **80% CLICKS**. The ultimate goal was to reduce the number of highway deaths and the number and severity of injuries that are at least partly attributable to the lack of occupant restraint use.

Through the Traffic Safety Education Department, the 80% CLICKS project utilized a *community interorganizational system of networking*. The schools, health, police, student, workplace, community, and special project systems were accessed. The central organizing role was assigned to the Traffic Safety Police Advisory Committee composed of municipal and Royal Canadian Mounted Police (RCMP) officers.

The immediate objective of the campaign was to raise the safety belt wearing rate in British Columbia from a pre-test wearing rate of about 50 percent to 80 percent. As Gusfield (1986) has written, initiators of moral action typically want to help people achieve some kind of better status, as defined and promoted by an organization. The Insurance Corporation of British Columbia embraced the idea of a preferred sociality when they added the following objectives to the campaign:

- To establish a sense of pride and a positive sense of commitment on the part of British Columbians for becoming the first province of Canada to endeavor to achieve an 80 percent wearing rate by its citizens.
- To model for the citizens an identifiable approach to an issue that is positive, based on community ownership; to begin to establish the need for community committees.

The campaign thus represented a more broadly-based mission, which was: that the Insurance Corporation of British Columbia believes in community pride, commitment, and ownership of traffic safety issues. These motives illustrate devotion to a civic spirit. By being more civic-minded, it was hoped that individuals would broaden their perspectives on traffic safety and that they would thereby drink from the cup of achievement—that is, to be the first Canadian province to realize an 80 percent wearing rate. There is an assumed "elective affinity" between raising the safety belt wearing rate and achieving personal meaning through civic pride.

In an effort to establish control over the definition of the mission objectives, the traffic safety employees patterned a background scenario built on research. An information package was organized for British Columbia citizens which legitimized the need for a major campaign:

> British Columbia's safety belt legislation was passed in October, 1977, and became enforceable in November, 1977. Shortly thereafter, a public campaign was initiated which resulted in a predictable high of 72 percent usage rate. In 1982, a safety belt survey showed that the usage rate had declined to between 40 and 50 percent. Raising wearing rates and maintaining them with or without legislation has always been a difficulty in British Columbia as in many other parts of Canada and the U.S.A. Realizing that failure to wear safety belts increases the chance of being severely or fatally injured, it is suggested that every attempt be made to increase the British Columbia usage rate.

An obvious consequence of a successful campaign is the enforcement of existing rules. This helps further institutionalize an organization's mission. If people witness the police rigorously checking vehicle occupants for safety belt wearing, they will be more inclined to respect the moral authority underlying a campaign. That is, they will recognize that the enforcement and punishment inflicted on people who were not buckled is real, under the formal endorsement of the state. To keep people aware about external reprisals, the Insurance Corporation encouraged the police to accomplish the following activities in a five-day period:

- 3,396 members in police detachments were involved in all matters pertaining to the crusade.
- 1,465 police officers participated in road checks during the time of the crusade.
- 208 auxiliary police were involved.
- 3,500 hours were spent on roadchecks during the crusade.
- 15,637 safety belt charges were issued to British Columbia citizens in a five-day period.
- 2,724 written warnings were issued to British Columbia citizens in a five-day period.

To support the police road checks, members of the Traffic Safety Education Department engaged in the following activities:

- 13,363 letters were sent.
- 136 media releases, radio interviews, television interviews were completed.
- 1,310 telephone calls relating to the campaign took place.
- 251 occupant restraint television advertisements were shown.

- 182 local committee meetings were held as part of the community interorganizational model.
- 413 presentations and visits took place.
- 50 safety belt convincer demonstrations took place.
- 814,399 pieces of mail were distributed.
- The Schools Program conducted a safety belt curriculum project for the 2,000 elementary schools.
- The Health Program conducted an infant and child restraint use television campaign.
- The Workplace Program conducted a pilot taxicab safety belt project.
- The Police Program conducted a pilot city media and enforcement project.
- The Special Projects program conducted student conferences and crash simulator convincer demonstrations.
- The Community Projects program published traffic safety newsletters.
- All in all, approximately forty projects on safety belt use were completed by the Traffic Safety Education Department.

So a campaign, representing a mission, was born. For 15 days, from May 20 to June 4, 1983, British Columbians were bombarded with messages, programs, and police actions. Persuasion, education, and enforcement tactics were used to influence and even coerce people to wear safety belts. And, in order to judge the extent to which people converted to the message, a province-wide roadside survey was undertaken at the end of the campaign.

Based on 18 interviewing hours at 28 provincial jurisdictions with a total of 5,660 drivers and 3,340 passengers, the following major provincial findings were reported:

- 67 percent of all occupants were using some form of restraint (a 12-percent increase from December, 1982).
- 73 percent of drivers were wearing a safety belt (a 13-percent increase from December, 1982).
- All age groups increased **except** the 6- to 15-year-olds, who already had the lowest incidence of usage; 74 percent of those under age 6 were wearing a restraint but "proper" usage was not determined.
- The most experienced drivers had the highest rate of compliance with the safety laws.
- Only five percent of all drivers claimed never to wear a restraint.
- 25 of the 28 jurisdictions showed an increase among drivers, while 22 showed an increase among all occupants.
- On average, the jurisdictions previously showing the lowest usage rate gained the most (B.C. Research, 1983, pp. 28-29).

Further breakdowns and specific statistical results were provided. But what is of significance to the campaign is the extent to which people converted to the campaign's overall goal. An answer to the query was provided. At checkpoints, if motorists were observed to be wearing restraints, they were asked how often they wore one and what was the main reason they were wearing a belt at that moment. The findings are represented in figure 10.

**Figure 10**
**Reasons for Wearing a Safety Belt**

| Reasons | Always wear (88%) | Was wearing then but not always (12%) |
|---|---|---|
| Campaign (e.g., roadblocks, tickets, etc.) | 1 | 9 |
| Safety/common sense | 57 | 31 |
| Compliance with law | 24 | 36 |
| Habit | 12 | 10 |
| Fear of being trapped or unsafe | 2 | 1 |
| Other specific (e.g., to set an example) | 3 | 9 |
| Other non-specific (e.g., no reason) | 1 | 4 |

Based on the above findings, the researchers concluded that:

> Only one in eight (12.5%) of the drivers who were wearing a belt said they did not always wear one, and most of those said they wore a belt most of the time. This group mentioned rather more specific reasons for wearing a belt at that time than others. In particular, 10 percent of them mentioned something specific to the various campaign components (e.g., roadblocks, fines, school programs, etc.). "Other specific" reasons tended to be similar to "I (or a friend/relation) was in an accident when I needed it" (B.C. Research, 1983, p. 23).

Overall, it was found that 10 percent of the drivers and passengers interviewed (both belted and unbelted) indicated a sharing in the campaign's objective. They buckled up because of the province-wide series of activities. Whether we believe that the gains made due to such organized events are in fact satisfactory, depend on the perspective from which we view the objectives and outcomes of the mission.

# The Second Campaign

The second campaign of note occurred four years after the first. From August 24 to September 14, 1987, the Insurance Corporation of British Columbia again initiated a province-wide movement to increase the overall provincial safety belt wearing rate. The focus was not so much on community programs as it was on media and promotion. The contours of media were television, radio, newspaper, and social exchange. A province-wide safety belt survey preceded the campaign to establish pre-existing wearing levels.

Within the free market of ideas, members of the Corporation advocated views of safety belt wearing they believed to represent truth. "The best test of truth," Justice Oliver Wendell Holmes wrote, "is the power of thought to get itself accepted in the competition of the market." In the case of the traffic safety mission, the market is composed of beliefs and ideas.

Previous research found that people who do not wear safety belts most often do not do so on short trips and at low speeds. Traffic safety personnel made such people the primary targets for the campaign. Secondary audiences were hard-core non-wearers. It was the traffic safety people's intention to paint a realistic picture of safety belt wearing risk. The most convenient approach for tapping the ideas market was to utilize television, radio and newspapers.

The television commercials were developed to portray the perspective of the mission. In the mid 1970s, Transport Canada designed a series of television ads which symbolically represented the risk of injury resulting from a crash in which the occupant was unrestrained. In video tape 1, the symbol is a pumpkin being squashed by a truck tire, in tape 2 the symbol is a coconut smashed in a press, and in tape 3 the symbol is eggs dropped in a carton. The text accompanying the ads was changed to be more relevant to the British Columbia scene. The text was:

**Tape 1**
Some people believe it's better to get thrown clear in a car crash, but at 50 km/h, that's the speed you will be doing when you hit the concrete or lighting pole or maybe you are just lying there stunned on the road. Now the best place to be in a car crash, is in the car . . . with your seatbelt buckled to hold you there. Think about it. If you're not wearing a seatbelt, what's holding you back?

**Tape 2**
People who don't wear seatbelts for city driving don't understand they can't brace themselves against the force of a low-speed accident. Let's do a demonstration. If you crash at 50 km/h, the force with which you and your coconut hit the dash is several

thousand pounds . . . something like that, and it all happens within seven-tenths of a second. Want to see it again? Brace yourself, think about it, if you're not wearing a seatbelt, what's holding you back?

**Tape 3**

When you're traveling along the road in your car at 50 km/h and you crash, you crash around too and you get hurt by the steering wheel or the windshield. But, if you wear seatbelts they restrain your movement in the car and reduce your chances of serious injury by up to 50 percent. Think about it . . . if you're not wearing a seatbelt, what's holding you back?

The copy-points for the safety belt wearing crusade illustrate how the Insurance Corporation of British Columbia dealt with a problem. Through the interpretation and life-engendering illustrations of risk, safety belt non-wearers were to shift their standards and wear a belt on a short trip or in a low-speed traffic situation. The copy-points were thus written:

1. In a crash at just 50 km/h, the same speed you drive on your way to the store . . . you'll hit the steering wheel or the dash, usually with your face, head, and upper body, with a force of several **thousand** pounds . . . unless you're wearing your safety belt.

2. If you're involved in a collision at just 50 km/h, and you're **not** wearing your safety belt, you'll slam into the steering wheel or the dash with the same impact as a fall from a three-storey building.

3. In a crash at 16 km/h . . . roughly the same speed you drive in a shopping centre parking lot . . . your head and upper body will hit the dash or the steering wheel with the same force you'd face by trying to catch a 200-pound (110 kg) weight dropped from seven feet above.

4. Imagine what would happen to you if you ran face first, full speed into a steel lamp post. The same thing can happen to you in a low-speed parking lot crash if your face and head collide with the inside of your car.

5. Two-thirds of all the people hurt in British Columbia traffic crashes each year are traveling on city streets at 50 km/h or less.

6. When you're in a car crash at only 50 km/h, there is no chance to brace yourself. It will take you just 1/100 of a second to hit the steering wheel or shift lever . . . the dash, the windshield, the roof, the windshield frame . . . or someone else in the car. Most of the time you hit your head or your chest with a force of several **thousand** pounds.

The campaign was built on the belief that citizens who do not wear safety belts are not fully informed or do not understand the meaning of the information they have. After hearing the ads, individuals can no longer excuse themselves from responsibility by claiming that they did not know about risk. Traffic safety personnel made sure that passengers and drivers could not claim failure to foresee the consequences of their safety belt non-wearing behaviors. Standards were invoked to influence non-wearers to adopt acceptable safety behaviors. A code was imposed for people to observe while traveling in a vehicle.

Precisely because the traffic safety personnel believed so strongly in the justifications of safety belt wearing and the need to increase the wearing rate, they linked with a series of networks to distribute promotional materials. They distributed materials to corporate and public health offices, medical clinics, police detachments, schools, fast-food restaurants, supermarkets, gas bars, insurance agencies, and taxis. In addition, fact-sheets, litter bags, bookmarks, two-way window decals, infant-child restraint installation instructions, and posters were designated for shopping centre malls, volunteer organizations, festivals, border crossings, car rental agencies, recreation centres, and summer student, youth-organized programs, among others.

Through the use of such strategies, the campaign was established to correct the wrongs of vehicle-occupant safety behavior. An absolute ethic paved the way: safety belt non-wearing is truly and totally wrong without qualification, and any legitimate means are justified to increase the wearing rate. The traffic safety workers were fervent in their belief that their mission was a righteous one.

How effective was the 1987 campaign in changing safety belt wearing behavior, at least, in the short-term? In thirteen jurisdictions where "before and after" surveys were conducted, the results were as follows:

- Twelve out of the 13 jurisdictions had an increase in safety belt wearing rate;
- In nine of these 12 jurisdictions, the increase was significant at the 0.05 level or better.

In addition, there was evidence to suggest that the increases in restraint use were related to the level of police activity.

In ten out of the twelve jurisdictions where a positive effect was noted, it was possible to assess the level of police activity within the local community. This was expressed in terms of the number of safety belt and child restraint-related charges laid during the course of the campaign. Since all the jurisdictions began with wearing rates at the 70% to 80% level, it is reasonable to assume that a unit of enforcement should have had roughly the same effect in each of them. Also, since the bulk of the publicity effort was province-wide in scope and all communities were exposed through television, radio and print media, it is reasonable to expect that differential effects of the campaign would be most related to the number of units of police enforcement applied.

The number of vehicle occupants likely to be on the road at any given time was considered to be proportional to the number of insured vehicles in each jurisdiction, multiplied by an average occupancy factor of 1.2. The estimated number of new wearers created by the campaign was then assumed to be the number of vehicle occupants multiplied by the change in percentage wearing between before-and-after surveys.

Figure 11 shows that the number of additional wearers was proportional to the number of units of enforcement (safety belt charges), and that the average ratio of new wearers to charges (as a measure of police effort) was just over seven. In other words, the effort by police represented by laying one charge created seven new safety belt wearers, at least for the duration of the campaign.

**Figure 11**
**Results of a Safety Belt Campaign in 10 Jurisdictions**

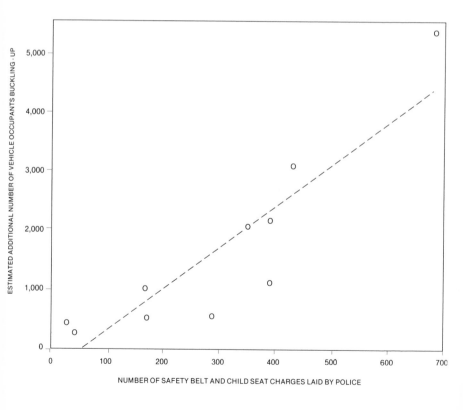

ESTIMATED ADDITIONAL NUMBER OF VEHICLE OCCUPANTS BUCKLING - UP

NUMBER OF SAFETY BELT AND CHILD SEAT CHARGES LAID BY POLICE

Comparing the results of the 1983 and 1987 campaigns, it is possible to see fairly dramatic evidence of the leveling-off effect alluded to at the beginning of this chapter. The so-called "law of diminishing returns" is clearly illustrated in terms of the results achieved for what were, as an order of magnitude, similar levels of effort. With a base of 55% wearing, the results were substantial (a 12-percentage point jump) but when the baseline was at 78% (in 1987) a similarly high level of publicity and enforcement effort produced only a four-percentage point rise. Such a phenomenon should be expected and thus the benefit/cost of undertaking large-scale safety belt campaigns must always be assessed as a function of the existing restraint use level.

The people served by moral activists may either accept or reject the social dominance of reformers. The extent to which they agree is based on the extent to which the reform denies, through enforcement, the legitimacy of their previous lifestyles. If there is a feeling of declining status intensified by enforcement and message, counter-morality rationales are developed and invoked. It becomes a struggle to maintain and affirm resistance. Truth is relative. Lowered self-esteem may become a rallying cry for the need for self-expression. Ill tempers may pervade. Individuals find, in their recipient roles as targets for reform tactics, perceptions of their status as rejection. They fight for respect in a way that is symbolic and significant.

In the case of safety belt wearing, the most obvious counter-strategy is not to wear safety belts. The hope is that participants do not encounter a police roadblock which may penalize this behavior. Others blaze into a roadcheck and defiantly accept the fine. The final verdict for them would be the courtroom. A second counter-strategy is to position the safety belt in such a way that it would look as though they were properly buckled up. The intent is symbolically to retain a sense of free will within the broad movement of a crusade. (There is also a sense of "winning"—i.e., they have beaten the system and remained undetected!)

If we search through the series of accounts that were given by self-proclaimed occasional or frequent safety belt non-wearers, we become aware of the emotional intensity underlying counter-beliefs and strategies.

After the 1987 crusade was over, 15,123 vehicle occupants were observed and interviewed at roadside stops throughout British Columbia. Although 94 percent responded that they **always** wore safety belts, the recorded observations showed a total of only 82 percent. Obviously, for some, "always" did not include the time that they were observed.

The occupants were asked the main reason for using a restraint. Figure 12 indicates responses to the frequency question, "always or sometimes wear seatbelts."

**Figure 12**
**Reasons for Using Restraints**

| Reasons | Always Wear N = 6,924 (%) | Sometimes wear N = 398 (%) |
|---|---|---|
| Safety/common sense | 60 | 33 |
| Compliance with the law | 20 | 31 |
| Habit | 15 | 13 |
| Children demand it | <1 | 2 |
| Warning buzzer/light | <1 | 3 |
| Social pressure | <1 | 2 |
| Setting an example for children | <1 | 1 |
| Experience in previous accidents | 2 | 1 |
| Company policy | <1 | <1 |
| Safety belt campaign | <1 | <1 |
| Other | <1 | 12 |

Other reasons cited for safety belt wearing, albeit by only a few individuals, included: I remembered to put it on; I feel more comfortable wearing it; insurance savings; advertised police roadblocks; afraid of being fined; I was trained that way; I wear it only on long distance and highway driving; I wear it in small cars; I'm scared of my driving; and there are a "bunch of idiots on the road."

Similarly, those people who were observed as not wearing a restraint were asked about frequency of usage and reasons for not wearing a restraint at the time of observation. Sixty-two percent claimed they wore a restraint more than half the time, nine percent about half the time, eight percent less than half the time, and 22 percent hardly ever or never. The main reasons are shown in figure 13.

## Figure 13
### Reasons for Not Wearing a Restraint

| Reasons | Sometimes wear $N = 1,230$ (%) | Never wear $N = 325$ (%) |
|---|---|---|
| Short trip | 45 | N/A[1] |
| Forgot/in a hurry | 30 | N/A |
| Belt uncomfortable; nuisance | 6 | 48 |
| In town; only wear on highway | 4 | N/A |
| I was wearing it (denial) | 8 | < 1 |
| Belt does not work | 2 | 7 |
| Medical certificate | 1 | 2 |
| Freedom of choice | N/A | 9 |
| Pregnant | < 1 | N/A |
| Fear of being trapped or burned; unsafe | N/A | 5 |
| Don't believe they help (non-specific) | N/A | 9 |
| Other | 3 | 19 |

[1] N/A means that this reason was not precoded since it did not make sense in the context of the specific question.

Nine percent of those who stated they never wore belts cited "freedom of choice," as their reason, and 14% lacked confidence in belt utility, but by far the largest proportion (48%) used "discomfort" as an explanation. Seven percent admitted to having inoperable restraints. Those who insisted that they sometimes wore their belts had a markedly different pattern of reasoning for not wearing on the trip in question. Mainly, they simply forgot or felt that their short exposure justified non-use. Fully 8%, however, apparently found it necessary to deny the observational evidence outright.

For those "sometime wearers," there was evidently an element of embarrassment in being caught without a belt on. They wished to make it clear that their current situation was not typical—they didn't reject the utility of belts per se—only the circumstances in which they were useful. The small group of full-time non-wearers were not excusing an aberrant behavior. They were expressing their low opinion of safety belt utility generally. Belts are so useless, in their opinion, that the potential benefits are outweighed by the disbenefit of minor discomfort.

Other reasons cited for not wearing safety belts included: not used to them; too lazy; never developed the habit; not in own car/new car; no safety belts in the car/truck; good driver/drive professionally; children not in car; not necessary for short trips; just took it off on the way into the lot; only on poor roads, not on quiet streets; previous experience in accidents when it didn't help or would have made things worse; and not worried/don't care.

## Attitudes Toward Safety Belt Campaign

Drivers were asked whether campaigns should be conducted to increase the use of safety belts. Two-thirds (67 percent) responded "yes" while only 24 percent said "no." The remaining nine percent indicated either a "qualified" yes (usually saying it depends on costs) or they said they did not know. Those who were not wearing a safety belt were less likely to respond yes (56 percent) compared to those wearing a safety belt (69 percent). Females were more likely to respond yes (71 percent) than were males (63 percent).

Many people argued in favor of missions and campaigns. Their positions extended to specific topics or issues. The following comments made by interviewees illustrate special interest in campaigns:

- Campaigns should be directed at children.
- There should be campaigns for use of car lights in the daytime.
- There should be campaigns against drunk driving.
- There should be educational campaigns giving driving tips.

The question on who should be responsible for mounting such campaigns produced a series of suggestions. We have listed a few of the recommendations most often mentioned:

- Oil companies and gas stations.
- Car manufacturers/safety belt makers.
- The media.
- Motor vehicle department/drivers' license bureaus.
- Safety councils/other service clubs.
- Ministry of Health.
- Mother and parent groups.
- Private companies.
- Liquor board.
- Communities.
- Student groups.
- Life insurance companies.
- **Not** by the government or police.

From those suggesting that mission backed campaigns were not necessary, the following reasons—representing the general array of responses—were cited:

- Everyone who is going to wear safety belts is already doing so.
- If they are not wearing them by now, they never will.
- Wearing safety belts should be a matter of free choice.
- Campaigns are a waste of time and money.

The increasing use of organized missions toward safety belts is beginning to make an impact on citizens. We often hear citizens tell of people defined as traffic disorderlies needing to be corrected in their errant way through campaigns mounted by responsible organizations or institutions. The ultimate illustration of people's views on traffic safety campaigns is drinking and driving.

In our interviews with observed wearers and non-wearers, we asked the drivers about the effectiveness of ads in reducing drinking-driving behavior. They expressed abundant faith in the efficacy of ads, 70% being convinced of their ability to impact the incidence of impaired driving.

The main reason they thought ads to be effective appeared to be a belief that the public only needed to be made aware; then, appropriate change would follow. Their ideas to promote such awareness with ads tended towards "shock" situations—plenty of blood and grieving relatives, although a significant proportion felt that ads could never be as tough and effective as police enforcement and would not likely influence the small group of problem drivers who are responsible for most of the unsafe driving.

Gusfield (1986) considered the emergence of an anti-drinking-and-driving movement as politically important because of groups like Mothers Against Drunk Drivers (MADD). It seems that a safety belt wearing movement also has the consent of a significant percentage of the public, in some part, due to crusading organizations.

# CHAPTER 12

# OUR BELIEFS ABOUT OTHERS' BELIEFS

Imagine an earth-bound observer from another planet. For him, traffic safety researchers would seem to constitute a group of persons whose business it is to construct slides of reality concerning traffic issues. At any specific time they make counts, examine cars, speak to people and make notes. They then take the products of these actions and organize, tabulate, graph, summarize and symbolize them (Schwartz and Jacobs, 1979). Finally a standardized, formatted explanation is presented.

When safety belt wearing rates are published in the news media and in learned journals, the findings are given as an actual inventory of the real world of driving. Numbers are assigned to qualitative observations. The wearing rate for a certain city, province or state becomes an authoritative "$X$." As a given truth, the cry then goes out that the "wearing rate" should at most be raised and at least maintained.

Based on our own studies we find that researchers' portrayal of safety belt wearing is a fuzzy picture of "what is really going on out there." The picture is fuzzy because laypersons have their own practical reasons for behaving as they do. Vast differences in circumstances, locations, times of day, and moods mitigate against any consistent notation system. They certainly pervade against any single determination of a given number of people wearing safety belts across all times and locations.

Motorists and passengers who do not wear safety belts for any reason are often judged by traffic safety personnel to be deviant and careless. Furthermore, based on broad categorizations in research studies, safety belt non-wearers are typecast as individuals who are unsafe in a variety of circumstances and situations. We have seen, however, that absolute categorizations of "wearers" and "non-wearers" are inappropriate. Even good drivers who are regular belt users admit to occasions or circumstances where normal practices are suspended. Thus, while such generalizations may be useful to researchers in understanding broad aspects of behavior within large groupings of drivers, they are not readily communicable or identifiable to individual citizens.

Modern societies are not simple organizations in which everyone agrees on what the rules are and how they are to be applied in specific situations (Becker, 1963b). Everyday rules of traffic, for example, are negotiated daily along social, class, ethnic, occupational, economic, cultural, and moral lines. Decisions are made daily in the traffic environment which may disagree with formal standards of road propriety but which respond to what is considered necessary and right. The police, traffic safety personnel and other officials see it differently.

Rose and Prell (1955) established that a strong belief evident in authorities' minds is that many or most rules are generally agreed to by all members of a society. However, empirical research on a given rule generally reveals variation in people's attitudes. Formal rules, enforced by some specifically constituted groups, often differ from those actually thought appropriate by many people. So, decisions not to wear safety belts that are made on the basis of certain circumstances may not hold true to different driving or social situations. Decisions of the people who engage in driving behaviors are likely to be quite different from those people who condemn them.

Traffic safety professionals believe that once people "acquire" the habit, they will break through past safety belt wearing inertia. For example, Evans (1987) suggested that encouraging the development of safety-oriented conventions or habits—like those adopted for personal hygiene—rather than encouraging drivers to constantly choose the safest behaviors, is the most promising approach to reducing risky driving behavior. This may even be effective with drivers who cause many road crashes due to their reluctance to follow the mainstream social driving norms.

Television ads have been designed to convince us to get into the habit of buckling up. Researchers have adopted habit as an interview response category for safety belt research.

Habit is supposed to carry weight. Unfortunately, habit has been oversimplified as a self-evident explanation with little structural support. All actions that are repeated frequently become cast into patterns, which may then be reproduced with an economy of effort. They become embedded as routines in people's ways of thinking. This carries important psychological repercussions. Decisions are no longer thought through on an informed basis. Undeliberated and unreflected actions become the modus operandi.

Habitualized driving behavior, in its pure sense, does not allow for motorists' analyses of particular social and vehicular relationships on the road. If attention were paid to the road circumstances, certain habits might need to be altered to accommodate the changing traffic situations. Unfortunately, habitual responses to demands made by certain groups carry strong implications of control and authority. Drivers are controlled for safety by establishing predefined patterns of conduct for them. Prediction is enhanced, and self-motivated thought about specific matters is diminished.

A popular traffic safety belief is that as more people acquire the habit of buckling up, the greater will be the reduction in personal risk. It can significantly reduce the severity of driver and passenger injuries when road crashes occur. Risk has been considered to be an objective phenomenon.

Psychological research on risk—with its emphasis on risk perception—has been directed toward measuring risk judgments, defining risk-relevant variables, and attempting to understand the factors that make a given level of risk acceptable to particular people.

Risk, however, is in fact a complex mental activity which is not context-free. MacMillan (1975) observed the relevance of a sociological approach to understanding road-user behavior. He noted that in other spheres of social activity, persons, groups, actions and events do not pop into existence suddenly but have a history. So it is in road traffic. There is a process whereby circumstances of the traffic environment arise that must be studied, if behavior in that environment is to be understood. This leads to the point of view that driving is not really a discrete behavior and therefore must be studied within its full social context. Some of the diverse variables included in this context include society's attitudes toward motoring offences (e.g., each driver's social experience and each driver's experiences while interacting with other drivers on the road and other occupants of his own vehicle, to name a few).

The humans within the traffic environment are more than vehicle drivers, passengers and pedestrians. Each of these groups is composed of subpopulations defined by variables such as age, sex, socioeconomic status, social roles, social abilities, cultural background and reasons for being in the traffic environment. In short, they are as diverse as society itself by its fullest definition and some of these other dimensions of social identity are relevant to any discussion on risk.

People engage in rule-governed behavior while driving. These rules pertain to experience of what works, to meaning of self-image, or to relationships with other people. To abide by the social and informal rules of behavior, drivers may experience safety belt non-wearing as normal, natural or self-evident. They define risks in a social sense, not a technical one. As is commonly understood, deliberate risk is subjective in the sense that it is only possible if some danger is believed to exist, independent of whether or not it actually does exist. Social and cultural contributions to what is perceived as risk, and the fact that any particular driver's perception of risk might vary from day to day and from situation to situation are major contributors to a comprehensive understanding of risk.

The beliefs about habit formation and reduction in risk are tied to the belief in law and order. Enforcement-based countermeasures are considered to be effective strategies to increase safety belt wearing and to produce safety gains. Behavior is controlled through a state management approach. The enactment of safety belt wearing laws and enforcement is considered to be a fruitful approach for reducing exposure to risk.

We believe that behavior is only a symptom; it is the surface manifestation of what is going on inside a person. The causes of behavior lie in people's beliefs, feelings, understandings, hopes, values and perceptions (Combs, 1979). They influence the things people do or do not do. Permanent changes in behavior require alteration in human perceptions. Understanding the personal view of behaviors, like safety belt wearing, is a preferable way for dealing with people's actions.

Although there is no doubt that the management philosophy often works to increase safety belt wearing in certain jurisdictions, still people's belief systems are not changed in connection with the changed behavior. This is because:

- Since the causes of behavior lie within the person, they cannot be directly manipulated or changed. Outsiders can only influence, facilitate, or help changes to happen by the ways they themselves behave and the experiences they provide for the behaver.
- Since the causes of behavior lie within the person, they are under his or her control. They cannot be changed without some sort of co-operation from the person whose behavior is to be changed.
- Causes of behavior, like feelings, beliefs, understandings, attitudes, and values, do not change easily or quickly. The more important the perception in the value system of the behaver, the more difficult the process of change (Combs, 1979, p. 57).

By adopting the process of law enforcement, we force people to behave in a prescribed fashion. We do not really care how people feel or think about the matter; what we want is proper behavior. We will get it in an illusionary fashion depending on the continuing effectiveness of persuasion and coercion. However, we are unlikely to get understanding and commitment to the cause on a long-term basis. In a democracy, this requires a personal approach—one of education, communication, co-operation and support.

# CHAPTER 13

# PROMOTING SAFETY BELT USE: A BLUEPRINT FOR CHANGE

The text presented in the previous 12 chapters is based on the assumption that social behaviors or conduct are filled with human content. We cannot separate social existence from the circumstances and situations in which we find ourselves. Involvement within situation refers to the way we handle our activities and how we assess the kind of involvement we believe is appropriate. We are especially sensitive to the kind of behavior that visibly forms the principal current of involvement.

By focusing on the dynamics of motoring-related situations rather than on the generalized qualities of persons, we are shifting our lenses drastically. We are now concerned about rules of social behavior upon which motoring systems are built. We propose, therefore, that any serious attempt of addressing safety belt wearing requires insight on how forms, as well as contents, of motorists' social activities are used to create and sustain different actions within different situations.

The following list of conclusions and recommendations reflects the thesis that social behavior is influenced by situational variables.

- **Educational programs or traffic safety campaigns should be oriented toward traffic related situations in which people's commonsense interpretations may militate against wearing safety belts.** When these situations are clarified, traffic safety officials should address the rationale or content of people's perspectives as to why safety belt wearing is not undertaken.

- It must be recognized that there will always be a number of people who survive serious accidents relatively unscathed even though they were not restrained and, also, some people who are injured in what seem to be relatively moderate-speed impacts even though belted. **Education programs must be designed to counteract misleading impressions of personal risk which the publicizing of such events inevitably creates.**

- To not wear safety belts may be unsafe but it is still structured on social rules that people use to carry on everyday life. Some behaviors leading to temporary unbuckling are not necessarily symptomatic of wrong attitudes so much as being a momentary, logical restructuring of priorities. **Specific education messages should therefore be geared toward the commonsense interpretations which people apply to different situations in the vehicle.**

Properly designed messages should not degrade people's cultural or social norms, which underly their logic for not wearing safety belts. Rather, the messages should acknowledge the existence and meaning of social rationality. Reasons for wearing safety belts should then be built on everyday reasoning.

- There is no one such group as the 20% (or whatever) safety belt non-wearers which roadside surveys refer to. Even though those who almost never or infrequently wear belts may have somewhat different "average" characteristics than those who frequently or almost always wear, the former group is not necessarily homogeneous enough to target reliably or effectively. At any given time, moreover, the potential population of non-wearers on the road will be far larger than the observed 20%. That this potential is seldom realized is a function of the "random" nature of wearer-non-wearer group shifts as a result of momentary decisions by individuals to temporarily suspend normal behavior patterns. **The campaign target may be specific socio-demographic groups or even all who travel in motor vehicles, but the messages should be geared towards the situations and/or contexts in which non-wearing most frequently occurs.**

- With respect to safety belt wearing campaign effectiveness, there is ample evidence that properly planned and executed restraint use campaigns, where high levels of police activity are supported by effective use of mass communications media, can be effective. The size of the effect, however, is highly dependent upon the prior level of restraint use. **Thus as wearing increases, increasingly more effort is required to produce the same level of effect and it is questionable whether wearing rates of close to 100% are actually achievable through such means alone. Such a consideration must be borne in mind when planning the assignment of resources to safety belt campaigns.**

- In many North American jurisdictions, safety belt wearing laws have been enacted. In many more, laws are being drafted for near future implementation. The credibility of a law is its universal application. **We suggest therefore, that safety belt wearing laws should be applied equally to all people including those in legal authority.** Because people perceive their own non-wearing as rational, sanctioned non-wearing by certain groups is considered by the same people as reinforcement or legitimization of their non-wearing logic. Also, commitment to the safety belt wearing law is reduced when there are "except for" clauses.

- It is not unusual to witness safety belt messages promoting the development of the safety belt wearing habit. However, habit has a connotation of consistency and commitment which is, from our results, not necessarily present in safety belt wearing. **We recommend, therefore, that safety belt wearing messages be designed to maintain acceptable wearing levels for different situations. To depend on habits for wearing maintenance may not be, in the long run, productive. Also, regardless of the current level of measured use, there will probably always be a need for enforcement/education campaigns to maintain acceptable levels.**

When we attend a baseball game on a warm Sunday afternoon we sit back in our T-shirt and shorts with some refreshments. At a Sunday afternoon symphony we dress formally, sit attentively in our assigned seats, and wait for an official break before we have a modest glass of refreshment. The race track, backyard, courthouse, tennis court and so forth require, nay demand, social behaviors that help sustain definitions of their uniqueness as situations. We have accepted and engaged in these behaviors for years as have our forebearers. If someone were to tell us that a change in behavior is to be enforced based on a different rationality, we would, in all likelihood, refer to our comfort zone of traditional rules of conduct and social priorities.

We should accept the contextual sense-making rationale when we discuss safety belt wearing. It is not so much the case that this "type" of driver wears a safety belt while that "type" does not. Depending on the circumstances the wearer becomes a temporary, nevertheless visible, non-wearer. The reverse is also true. So, the contextual perspective becomes the meaningful scheme for safety belt wearing sense-making. After all, this is only common sense, since every day we do things based on "of-course" assumptions we have for each situation.

**"... Never Say Always."**

# LIST OF FIGURES

# BIBLIOGRAPHY

Adams, J. **Risk and Freedom**. Cardiff, England: Transport Publishing Projects, 1985.

Aquinas, St. Thomas. **Summa Theologica**. Volume II, Part 1-11, Question 90, Article 4, p. 995.

Asch, S.E. "Studies of Independence and Conformity. A Minority of One Against a Unanimous Majority." **Psychology Monographs** 70, no. 9 (1958).

B.C. Research. **Restraint Usage '87. Post-Campaign Results**. A report submitted to the Traffic Safety Education Department, Insurance Corporation of British Columbia, North Vancouver, BC, October 30, 1987.

———. **Restraint Usage in British Columbia During 80% CLICKS!** A report submitted to the Traffic Safety Education Department, Insurance Corporation of British Columbia, North Vancouver, BC, July, 1983.

———. **Restraint Usage in British Columbia, June 3 and 4, 1982**. A report submitted to the Traffic Safety Education Department, Insurance Corporation of British Columbia, North Vancouver, BC, January 21, 1983.

———. **Restraint Usage in British Columbia, November 27– December 11, 1982**. A report submitted to the Traffic Safety Education Department, Insurance Corporation of British Columbia, North Vancouver, BC, January 21, 1983.

Becker, H. **Moral Entrepreneurs**. Glenco, IL: Free Press of Glencoe, 1963.

———. **Outsiders: Studies in the Sociology of Deviance**. New York: Free Press, 1963b.

Berger, P. **Sociological Work**. New York: Aldine Publishing Co., 1972.

Berger, P., and Berger, B. **Sociology: A Biographical Approach**. New York: Basic Books, 1975.

Berger, P., and Geer, B. "Participant Observation: The Analysis of Qualitative Field Data." **Human Organization Research**. Edited by Adams and Preiss. Homewood, IL: Dorsey Press, 1960.

Berger, P., and Luckmann, T. **The Social Construction of Reality**. Garden City, NY: Anchor Books, 1967.

Bierstedt, R. **The Social Order**. New York: McGraw-Hill, 1957.

Bragg, W.E. **Seat belts: "A good idea but they are too much bother."** Unpublished report prepared for the Ministry of Transport, Road and Motor Vehicle Safety Branch, Ottawa, ON, 1973.

Busek von, C.R.; Evans, L.; Schmidt, D.E.; and Wasielewski, P. "Seat Belt Usage and Risk Taking in Driving Behavior." **Accident Causation**. Warrendale, PA: Society of Automotive Engineers, Inc., February, 1980.

Combs, A.W. **Myths In Education**. Boston, MA: Allyn and Bacon, 1979.

Conrad, P. "The Discovery of Hyperkinesis: Notes On The Medicalization of Deviant Behavior." **Social Problems** 23 (1975).

Cooper, P.J. **The Estimation of Driver Population Statistics from Casualty Accident Data**. North Vancouver, BC: Insurance Corporation of British Columbia, 1985.

————. **The Relative Risk of Casualty Accident Involvement for Various Classes of Driver, Vehicle and Roadway in British Columbia**. North Vancouver, BC: Insurance Corporation of British Columbia, 1985.

Covello, U.; van Winterfeldt, D.; and Slovic, P. "Risk Communication: A Review of the Literature." **Risk Abstracts** (1987): 171-182.

Dreitzel, H. (ed.) **Recent Sociology**, no. 2. New York: MacMillan Co., 1970.

Durkheim, E. **Sociology and Philosophy**. London: Cohen and West, 1953.

————. **Rules of Sociological Method**. London: Cohen and West, 1952.

Emerson, J. "Behavior in Private Places: Sustaining Definitions of Reality in Gynecological Examinations." In H. Dreitzel (ed.), **Recent Sociology**, no. 2. New York: MacMillan Co., 1970.

Evans, L. "Factors Controlling Traffic Crashes." **Journal of Applied Behavioral Science** 23, no. 2 (1983): 201-218.

————. **Occupant Protection Device Effectiveness in Preventing Fatalities**. Warren, Michigan: General Motors Research Laboratories, 1987.

Evans, L., and Frick, M.C. **Seating Position in Cars and Fatality Risk**. Warren, Michigan: General Motors Research Laboratories, 1987.

Fagothey, A. **Right and Reason**. Saint Louis MO: C.V. Mosby Company, 1976.

Fhaner, G., and Hane, M. "Seat belts: factors influencing their use, a literature survey." **Accident Analysis and Prevention** 5 (1973).

Foote, N. "Concept And Method In The Study of Human Development." In M. Sherif and M.O. Wilson (eds.), **Emerging Problems In Social Psychology**. Norman, OK: Institute of Group Relations, 1957.

Garfinkel, H. **Studies in Ethnomethodology**. Englewood Cliffs, NJ: Prentice Hall, 1967.

Goffman, I. **Frame Analysis**. New York: Harper Colophan Books, 1974.

———. **Interaction Ritual**. New York: Anchor Books, 1967.

———. **The Presentation of Self in Everyday Life**. New York: Anchor Books, 1959.

Gurvitch, G. **The Social Frameworks of Knowledge**. New York: Harper Torchbooks, 1966.

Gusfield, J.R. **The Culture of Public Problems**. Chicago: University of Chicago Press, 1981.

———. "Social Structure and Moral Reform: A Study of the Women's Christian Temperance Union." **American Journal of Sociology** LXI (November, 1955).

———. **Symbolic Crusade**. 2nd ed. Urbana, IL: University of Illinois Press, 1966.

Hannah, T. **Some attitudinal, motivational and personality differences between seat belt users and non users**. Unpublished report prepared for Ministry of Transport, Road and Motor Vehicle Safety Branch, Ottawa, ON, 1975.

Hayakawa, S.I. **Language In Thought And Action**. New York: Harcourt, Brace and World, 1945.

Heron, R. **A Review of Three Studies Attempting to Relate Reported Seat Belt Usage to Seat Belt Attitudes and Other Variables**. Road and Motor Vehicle Traffic Safety Branch, Ministry of Transport, Ottawa, ON, 1975.

Insurance Institute For Highway Safety. "Status Report." Vol. 22, no. 13, December 5, 1987.

Jessor, R. "Problem-Behavior Theory, Health Promotion, and Risky Driving." Edited by R. Blackman, G. Brown, D. Cox, S. Sheps and R. Tonkin. In **Adolescent Risk Taking Behavior**, Young Driver Behavior Project. Vancouver, BC: University of British Columbia, 1985.

Jonah, B., and Lawson, J. "Safety belt use rates and user characteristics." **OECD Workshop on Effectiveness and Safety Belt Use laws**. Washington, D.C., November, 1985.

Kaplan, A. **The Conduct of Inquiry**. San Francisco: Chandler Publishing Co., 1964.

Kitterie, N. **The Right To Be Different**. Baltimore: John Hopkins University Press, 1971.

Leiss, W., and Krewski, D. "Risk Communication Process: A Review of Conceptual Models and Some Current Practices." Unpublished manuscript, April, 1987.

Lewin, K. **Field Theory In Social Science**. New York: Harper and Brothers, 1951.

Lonergan, B.J.F. **Insight: A Study of Human Understanding**. San Francisco: Harper and Row, 1957.

Lyman, S.M., and Scott, M. **A Sociology of the Absurd**. New York: Appleton-Century-Crofts, 1970.

———. "Coolness in Everyday Life." In M. Truzzi (ed.), **Sociology and Everyday Life**. Englewood Cliffs, NJ: Prentice-Hall, 1968.

MacMillan, J. **Deviant Drivers**. Hants, England: Saxon House, D.C. Heath Ltd., 1975.

McHugh, P. "A Common Sense Perception of Deviance." In H. Dreitzel (ed.), **Recent Sociology**, no. 2. New York: MacMillan Co., 1970.

McKay, H. "The Neighbourhood and Child Conduct." In K. Stoddart (ed.), **The Sociology of Deviance Book 1**. Richmond, BC: Open Learning Institute, 1979.

Mercer, W. "The Characteristics Of Night-Time Drivers in British Columbia." Victoria, BC: Ministry of Attorney General, 1982.

Merriam-Webster. **Webster's Ninth New Collegiate Dictionary**. Markham, ON: Thomas Allen & Son, 1986.

Morgan, J. "Who Uses Seatbelts?" **Behavioral Science** 12 (1967).

Morton, Brian. "Vancouver Survivor Didn't Use Seatbelt, Inquest Told." In **The Vancouver Sun**, April 30, 1987. Vancouver, BC: Pacific Press, 1987.

Nelson, G.D., and Moffit, P. "Safety Belt Promotion: Theory and Practise." **Accident Analysis and Prevention** 20, no. 1 (1988): 27-38.

O'Day, J., and Filkins, L.D. "Attitudes Toward Wearing Belts: A Survey of Michigan Drivers." **UMTRI Research Review** 14, no. 1 (1983): 1-8.

Ortega, Gasset Y. **Meditations on Quixote**. New York: Norton & Company, 1961.

Postman, N.; Nystrom, C.; Strate, L.; and Weingartner, C. **Myths, Men and Beer: An Analysis of Beer Commercials on Broadcast Television, 1987**. Falls Church, VA: AAA Foundation for Traffic Safety, 1987.

Reynolds, J.M. "The Medical Institution." In L.T. Reynolds and J.M. Haslin (eds.), **American Society: A Critical Analysis**. New York: David McKay, 1973.

Rose, A.M., and Prell, A.E. "Does the Punishment Fit the Crime? - A Study in Social Valuation." **American Journal of Sociology** LXI (1955) 247-259.

Rothe, J.P. (ed.). **Rethinking Young Drivers**. North Vancouver, BC: Insurance Corporation of British Columbia, 1987.

Ryan, W. **Blaming the Victim**. New York: Vintage Press, 1970.

Sanders, W.B. **The Sociologist As Detective**. New York: Praeger Publishing, 1976.

Sartre, J.P. **Existentialism and Humanism**. London: Methuen, 1946.

Schutz, A. **Collected Papers I: The Problem of Social Reality**. The Hague: Martinus Nijhoff, 1973.

———. **Collected Papers II: Studies In Social Theory**. The Hague: Martinus Nijhoff, 1971.

Schwartz, H., and Jacobs, J. **Qualitative Sociology**. New York: Free Press, 1979.

Simmel, G. **Conflict And The Web Of Group-Affiliations**. New York: Free Press, 1955.

Singer, P. **Practical Ethics**. Cambridge: Cambridge University Press, 1979.

Stern, A. **Sartre: His Philosophy and Existential Psychoanalysis**. New York: Dell Publishing Inc., 1967.

————. **The Search For Meaning: Philosophical Vistas**. Memphis: Memphis State University Press, 1971.

Stoddart, K. "The Fact Of Life About Dope." **Urban Life and Culture** 3, no. 2 (July, 1974): 179-204.

Thompson, M. "Aesthetics of risk: culture or context." **Societal Risk Assessment**, R.C. Schwing and W.A. Albers, eds., New York: Plenum Press, 1980.

Toennies, F. **Fundamental Concepts of Sociology**. New York: Random House, 1940.

Transport Canada. **The Design And Implementation Of A Seat Belt Education Program In Ontario**. Ministry of Transportation and Communication, Ontario, 1975.

Tussman, J. **Obligation and the Body Politic**. London: Oxford University Press, 1979.

Wagenaar A.; Streff F.; Molnar L.; Businski K.; and Schultz R. **Factors Related to Nonuse of Seat Belts in Michigan**. Ann Arbor, MI: Transportation Research Institute, University of Michigan, 1987.

Webb, G.R.; Bowman, J.A.; and Sanson-Fisher, R.W. "Studies of Child Safety Restraint Use in Motor Vehicles – Some Methodological Considerations." **Accident Analysis and Prevention** 20, no. 2 (1988).

Weber, M. **The Methodology of the Social Sciences**. Glencoe, IL: The Free Press, 1949.

Werner, W. "A Study of Perspective In Social Study." Unpublished Ph.D. thesis, University of Alberta, Edmonton, Alberta, 1976.

Williams, A.F. "Factors Associated With Seat Belt Use In Families." **Journal of Safety Research** 4, no. 3 (September, 1972).

Williams, E.B. and Malfetti, J.L. **Driving and Connotative Meanings**. Columbia: Teacher College Press, 1972.

Wiseman, J. **Stations of the Lost**. Chicago: University of Chicago Press, 1979.

Zaidel, D. "Risk, Driver Behaviour and Traffic Safety." **Evaluation 85: International Meeting On The Evaluation of Local Traffic Safety Measures**. ASSECAR, Arcueil, France, 1985.

Zukav, G. **The Dancing Wu Li Masters: An Overview Of The New Physics**. Toronto: Bantam Books, 1979.

# APPENDICES

# APPENDIX A: NOTES ON RESEARCH METHODOLOGY

## Introduction

The methodological tasks of this book have been to apprehend and reconstruct, as closely as possible, the perspectives of safety belt wearing and non-wearing from two very different social worlds—the world of everyday life and the world of empirical research. Special emphasis has been placed on the evaluative rules, which people use to reason through non-wearing behavior.

For too long, safety belt non-wearing behavior has had limited definition and description. As Williams (1972) and others have pointed out, no very compelling or useful explanations have emerged from the research. Much of the earlier research has looked at personality and demographic correlates of belt use, with some contradictory findings. Most of these findings, while they were interesting, were of very limited practical use in planning strategies to increase belt use (Transport Canada, 1975). They represented the theme that, "what's going on out there in traffic is whatever we, the traffic safety researchers, say is going on out there." Unfortunately, the traditional approaches never did tell us "what is really going on out there."

To get at the actual "goings on," we followed the basic Schwartz and Jacobs (1979) position that, "what's going on out there is what the actors say is going on out there." People live in their world. Who knows better than they what it is like and how it may best be described.

## People's Common Sense

We wanted to know what the motorists know, see what they see, and understand what they understand.

We endeavored to sense the important from the unimportant—social reality from within. To do so, we gathered their perspectives on the practicalities of everyday life. Perspective, as used in our book, reflects Becker and Geer's usage of the term in their classic study, *Boys in White*:

> We use the term "perspective" to describe a set of ideas and actions used by a group in solving collective problems. The content of a group's perspective includes a definition of the environment and the problems it presents as seen by group members, an expression of what members expect to derive from the environment, and the ideas and actions group members employ in dealing with the problem situation (1960; p. 280).

Most individuals proceed to do things on a pragmatic, piecemeal basis. Underlying the pragmatism is commonsense logic which reflects everyday rules used for real-life events. These rules are based on the practical, the social, and the immediate. They are the ingredients of life that needed uncovering.

Taylor (1981) suggested that a task analysis approach is not adequate for fully describing tasks such as "driving the family to the supermarket" or "driving to the airport to catch a plane" where the task is to arrive at the destination without mishap or accident. In such cases, the task is bounded by what is intended (goal destination) and what is not intended (mishap). This, the author points out, requires analysis of intentions, rules and expectations as well as an ergonomic analysis of the driving task. These factors bring in many schools of psychology and sociology. He argues that study of the rules governing driver behavior (i.e., personal rules related to risk and judgment and social convention rules related to social roles and peer group norms) are just as relevant to traffic safety as are traditional empirical research variables, if not more so.

# Selection Of Methods

To provide maximum data upon which we could offer a descriptive textual account of safety belt non-wearing, we engaged four major research methods. These methods—biographies, small group interviews, surveys, and aggregate data analysis—are described as follows.

## Biographies

Biographical accounts serve as empirical referents. They offer an invaluable source of data for gaining some insight into what it was that brought individuals to behave in a certain way at a certain time (Sanders, 1976). If done with a broad focus, researchers can uncover thoughts, emotions and social concerns which may have motivated certain behaviors.

For our endeavors we isolated two university sociology classes. The students—ranging widely in ages, experiences, fields of study and other demographic variables—were asked to write carefully thought-out accounts of their experiences with respect to safety belts. To attain full descriptions, the request was made as part of a course assignment. Two hundred submissions based on the following guidelines were received:

> Please describe an occasion when you did not wear safety belts when operating or riding in a motor vehicle. Also, indicate why you did not buckle up on this occasion.

More specifically, the following factors are noteworthy:

1. Both genders were roughly equally represented and the age range for informants was 18 to 45. The younger age groups (i.e., 20s), however, were somewhat overrepresented. This was not problematic: for one thing, concern was with activities and these do not appear to be age-specific; for another thing, the corpus of accounts contained reports of activities engaged in by persons from age 6 to age 86. Item 2 below should settle the question of age representation.

2. In order to ensure that the perspectives derived from the date were independent of any production cohort, they were discussed in eight focus groups of six participants each. Both genders and a variety of ages were represented. With few exceptions the perspectives were assessed as not attached to a particular cohort, age, or otherwise.

3. No informant was unable to provide an account; a fact which suggests that the occasional non-use of safety belts is common in the experience of local motorists and passengers. Indeed, many claimed they had difficulty in deciding "which one" of an array of possibilities to recount.

4. The lengths of the accounts varied from several paragraphs to elaborate mini-essays. Some informants provided descriptions on the experience of others in addition to their own.

### Validation Process

To help establish the extent to which the formulations analyzed from the accounts reflect people's intents, and to which the textual submissions reflect naturally occurring social behavior, we interviewed 48 random participants.

The small group interviews offered us opportunities to discuss at length about people's safety belt wearing behavior. The discussions helped pinpoint pertinent aspects of the written accounts, to expand the meaning of answers, and to establish the extent to which one set of data was consistent with another one.

## Small Group Interviews

Two sets of small group interviews were undertaken. Besides the 48 university subjects, we further interviewed 60 random motorists representing a variety of perspectives.

In the latter part of 1987, the Insurance Corporation of British Columbia became involved in a province-wide roadside safety belt wearing survey. Researchers observed motorists and interviewed them for information. A sample of subjects who were observed not to be wearing safety belts during the time of research were requested to participate in focus group discussions to be held later in the month.

Ten groups of six members per group located in four different geographical areas in British Columbia participated. The citizens were diverse in terms of age, gender and region of residence. Also they varied in the extent to which they wear safety belts on a regular basis. With the wide variation, we could retrieve aspects of the everyday, commonsense ideologies and rationalities that motorists and passengers invoke to support their "failure" to buckle up, whether it be on an occasional or persistent basis.

In each focus group, the investigator pursued the following themes:

1. When or if participants had occasion to remove their safety belts while driving or riding as a passenger.
2. If some seats in the vehicle are considered to be safer than others.
3. Probability of being in accidents.
4. Everyday risks people take while at home compared to risks in the car.
5. Exemption of wearing for certain classes of drivers.
6. Automobile and safety belt maintenance.
7. The media and reporting risks.
8. Laws, people's rights, and safety.
9. Perceptions on the technicality of safety belts.
10. Survival and safety belts.

Wiseman's (1979) timeless study on skid row had the following to say about the concept of validity which we believe is relevant to our study:

> . . . the validity problem is not whether the empirical indicators used to operationalize concepts are indeed valid representations of this phenomenon from an objective or scientific point of view (or even the so-called rational or reasonable man's point of view), **but whether or not the investigator has represented the social world of the actor as the actor himself sees it**. The agreement of an "objective" investigator as to whether this is the "real" (and not distorted) social world is moot, by definition. In this study one man's reality could be another man's gross distortion. The question of validity remains, however, only it must be interpolated for the purposes of this type of study as follows (emphasis added):
>
> 1. Do the social actors in question build the concepts and constructs of their daily social reality out of the same data that the investigator has gathered and with the same general forms emerging?

2.  How valid are the conclusions the investigator draws from the constructs he is using to depict this special social world he has selected to study (1979, p. 280)?

We recognize that by deciding to study the specific segment of reality pertaining to safety belt non-wearing, we give a subjective expression of choice. According to Zukav (1979), such a choice affects our perception of reality. We do not apologize for this. Any and all persons who carry attitudes are by nature prejudiced. In fact, the point of view that we can be without a point of view is a point of view. Our belief in life world description is nicely represented in the following quote:

> "Reality" is what we take to be true. What we take to be true is what we believe. What we believe is based upon our perceptions. What we perceive depends upon what we look for. What we look for depends upon what we think. What we think depends upon what we perceive. What we perceive determines what we believe. What we believe determines what we take to be true. What we take to be true is our reality (1979, p. 310).

To attain greater depth of understanding on matters of interest which arose from the group interviews we further interviewed 10 individuals who represented specific groups, ideologies or jurisdictions. This helped validate previous analysis plus it provided greater scope to everyday world descriptions as reflected in specific community groups.

## Safety Belt Non-User Survey

A survey was undertaken to gather and assemble data to help identify factors on why approximately 20% to 25% of British Columbia drivers do not wear safety belts on a regular basis. The survey consisted of the following three stages.

1. Observation of driver behavior.
2. Interviews with selected drivers.
3. Retrieving driver records.

### Observation of Driver Behavior

For six weeks, British Columbia-licensed vehicles were observed and recorded by a contracted research firm at seventeen sites in or near the city of Vancouver. The sites were divided according to highway and urban/suburban travel. For highway traffic sites, observers were located at points of exit and rest stops. Since the highway surveyed had few stops along a stretch of sixty miles (96 km) prior to the rest stop, the drivers observed would in all likelihood have either worn or not worn safety belts over a significant period of time. Because the highway was used for long trips and fast speeds (over 90 km/h), it was assumed that those observed unrestrained were, more likely than not, habitual non-wearers.

For the urban/suburban locations, different sites were observed on two consecutive days. The observation locations were at parking lots and park and ride locations where regular commuters congregate. The times of observation were from 7:30 a.m. to 9:30 a.m., Monday to Friday. For these sites the observation process was as follows:

Day 1

>For all cars entering the site the following was recorded:
>
>Vehicle licence (British Columbia only)
>Estimated driver age (three categories, for record retrieval purposes)
>Driver gender
>Safety belt use
>Headlight use

Day 2

>Drivers of vehicles matching Day 1 observations with respect to age, gender and belt use were requested to grant an interview at a time and place of their choice. Anonymity of the participants was stressed throughout the process.

Observers were careful to position themselves so as to be able to see into a slow-moving vehicle but not to be conspicuous to the drivers entering the parking lots or rest stops. Drivers should not have been aware of the initial observation process.

In British Columbia, the Motor Vehicle Act requires all vehicles of model year 1964 or later to be equipped with belts in the driver and outboard front passenger positions if the vehicle is to be operated on provincial highways.

Sample

The observational sites yielded a total sample of 391 usable records consisting of both wearers and non-wearers. Over one hundred and sixty of the records were complete in all respects. The drivers were interviewed on the second day of observation in the city or at a pause area on the highway. The British Columbia Motor Vehicle Department supplied the drivers' records and the insurance policy information.

**Interviews With Selected Drivers**

As outlined in the Day 2 descriptions, interviewers—without specifically knowing about the driver being a belt wearer or non-wearer—asked a series of questions of the driver. The anonymity of the status of each driver was assured because:

- The original observers did not do the latter interviews.
- The interviewers were located at different locations from the initial observers.
- The questions stressed traffic safety generally and not belt wearing behavior primarily.
- The interviewers selected people to be interviewed once they were away from their cars. Times for interviews subsequent to the observation were set.

It is important to note, therefore, that the drivers interviewed should not have been aware that they were selected on the basis of observed safety belt use. Such a factor is critical in assessing the subject refusal rates.

A questionnaire (24 main questions), provided by the Insurance Corporation of British Columbia, was administered by two interviewers. Since many of the questions were open-ended, the interviewers encouraged discussion of the topics introduced by each question. They then recorded brief summary-answers.

Each interview response was coded according to the principal theme(s) included in the answer. Two coders reviewed the entire data. Gross categories were refined a number of times to gain a tabular picture of phenomena. The data were entered into a computer and they were then tabulated and interpreted.

## Retrieving Driver Records

To obtain the official record for the drivers observed (consistent behavior), the British Columbia Motor Vehicle Department was provided directly by the research firm with a list of vehicle license numbers, together with the driver sex and age, or estimated age, for each. Entries on the list were identified by a serial number which was also recorded on the interview form where one was completed.

The records for drivers that could be identified were purged of personal information and combined with their respective interview forms, or with their respective field observations where no interview had been obtained. The final, anonymous data forms were then delivered to the Insurance Corporation of British Columbia.

A number of drivers could not be identified since only the registered owner of a vehicle would be associated with that vehicle in the official records. Drivers of company cars, for example, could not be identified through the plate number.

### Combining Data

The various data sources allowed us to compare features, characteristics and attitudes evident in safety belt wearers and non-wearers.

# Campaign Surveys

Province-wide pre and post safety belt wearing campaigns were carried out during mid-June, 1987, and mid-September, 1987. The September study was a replication of the June research except that the number of jurisdictions was increased from 13 to 28. A description of the methodology for the September, 1987, survey is thus provided.

## Jurisdictions

In view of the importance of the individual jurisdiction findings, the survey methodology was designed to maximize the utility of the local results, with rather less importance placed on procedures for obtaining the provincial aggregate. Twenty-eight jurisdictions were included. Of these, twelve were independent city detachments; five were autonomous RCMP units; eight were detachments selected to represent an RCMP Subdivision; and finally, three detachments which were part of the Vancouver RCMP Subdivision were considered to be autonomous for analysis purposes.

## Interview Sites

In general, the selected sites had the following characteristics:

- Representative of each jurisdiction with respect to urban, suburban, and highway driving.
- Representative of each jurisdiction with respect to socioeconomic levels and cultural mix.
- Representative with regard to driving purpose: service (shopping, dining out, doctor's visits, etc.), excursion (movies, parks, sports events, etc.), and commuter traffic.
- Natural stopping places (e.g., parking lots).
- Well lit in the evening and in a fairly well populated area (since interviewers worked alone).
- Arranged such that interviewers could observe vehicles as they approach parking spots so that restraint usage could be observed before the occupants unbuckled.
- Since interviewers were on foot, the lots were not too large; there had to be an identifiable territory they could cover and still obtain a reasonable number of observations.
- Fairly even (not too fast, not too slow) traffic flow.
- Where possible, the distance between sites within a jurisdiction was kept to a minimum to facilitate travel between them.
- Reasonably close to a main town.

Most sites were small-to-medium sized shopping malls or service stations. Occasionally, other types of site were used to represent a particular jurisdiction appropriately (e.g., factory, medical centre, or recreational parking lots).

## Survey Stints

Thirty-six hours of interviewing were conducted over a period of approximately three weeks from Wednesday, September 9 through Sunday, September 27, in each of the 28 jurisdictions. In a typical jurisdiction there were three sites: 12 hours were spent at each—four hours in the morning, afternoon, and evening. Two different sites were surveyed each day. This design ensured balance for unknown factors which could affect traffic patterns and usage rates.

## Sample

In total, 9,536 vehicles were sampled—an average of 341 in each jurisdiction. The actual number of interviews in each jurisdiction was, to some extent, arbitrary. On the basis of the budget available, each jurisdiction was assigned 36 interviewing hours and all but three received that full effort. The difference among jurisdictions in the quantity of data collected is primarily a function of the volume of traffic encountered at each site. The smallest number of interviews conducted in a particular jurisdiction was 174, where low traffic volumes existed and some scheduling difficulties occurred.

The 95% confidence intervals for restraint usage are dependent on the variation among sites. With the relatively high usage rates observed, confidence intervals on driver usage results are typically within $\pm$ 4% if random sampling is assumed. In practice, sampling is not purely random, and a judgment factor must be added to the confidence interval to account for the extent to which a representative sample was obtained.

The vehicles observed contained 15,342 occupants—an average of 548 in each jurisdiction. These numbers suggest average confidence intervals of $\pm$ 3% for total occupant usage rates.

The interview form is located in Appendix B.

## Analysis

During the week following the survey, each questionnaire was edited manually prior to keying. Further edits were conducted on the computer file. SPSS-X (Version 2.1) was used to conduct most of the analyses. S20/20 (a spreadsheet) was used to generate some of the tables.

Studies similar in methodological design were completed in 1982 and 1983. In the winter of 1982, 9,580 vehicles were sampled within 32 hours of interview time. In 1983, the assigned number of interview hours was 18. In total, 5,660 vehicles were sampled.

All province-wide survey studies not only addressed the extent to which vehicle occupants wore safety belts, but they also featured findings on who "always wears safety belts" (based on self admission), who "was wearing safety belts at the time of survey but does not always wear them" (based on self admission), and who "admittedly never wears them." To give further direction to the findings, data were provided on reasons underlying the three response categories previously outlined. The 1987 surveys also included questions and observations concerning daytime headlight use and retrofitting of centre, high-mounted brakelights.

## Aggregate Data Analysis

The accident data base employed was constructed using data from police-attended accidents occurring in 1986, matched with related information on claims and driver records. All injury-producing accidents in British Columbia are investigated by the police and, therefore, such crashes constituted the major portion of the data base. Since only 75% of the 1986 records could be reliably matched, the absolute numbers derived from the analysis do not match official (Motor Vehicle Department) records for that year. This is not important for our purposes, however, since the obtained sample size of about 65,000 drivers in police-attended crashes, having complete accident, vehicle, claim, and past driver record information provides ample scope for unbiased, meaningful comparisons amongst variables.

For the purpose of injury severity analysis and assessment of belt wearing, a subsample of 1,000 records was extracted from the data base. Five hundred of these were drivers judged by police not to have been buckled up at the time of the accident and who, in addition, had one or more past convictions for belt non-use. All of these vehicles were reported to be equipped with lap/shoulder restraints. A representative sample of 500 belted drivers (wearing during last accident and no prior safety belt convictions) was also extracted. Insurance claim files were consulted to confirm belt wearing categorizations and to provide accurate injury-level assessments.

# Ideal Types

To help describe the meaningful essential characteristics of safety belt wearing, we developed **ideal type** wearers and non-wearers. Through ideal type construction we attempt to resolve the question concerning how people's meanings about their acts can be identified by an observer in "objective conceptual categories." According to Kaplan, an ideal type:

> . . . specifies something with which the real situation or action is compared and surveyed for explication of certain of its significant components (1964, p. 83).

For the purpose of analysis we constructed the ideal types—"wearers" and "non-wearers." We defined them on the basis of controlled norms, conditions and assumptions. The social phenomena of safety belt wearing can better be clarified when ideal types are compared. Weber's comment nicely illustrates our intent:

> . . . to understand how a war is conducted, it is necessary to imagine an ideal commander-in-chief for each side . . . . Each of these commanders must know the total fighting resources of each side and all the possibilities arising therefrom of attaining the concretely unambiguous goal, namely, the destruction of the enemy's military power. On the basis of this knowledge, they must act entirely without error and in a logically 'perfect' way. For only then can the consequences of the fact that the real commanders neither had the knowledge nor were they free from error, and that they were not purely rational thinking machines, be unambiguously established (1949, p. 42)

As heuristic devices we can take the ideal types of wearer and non-wearer, compare and contrast them in order that similarities and differences in reference to the types can be established.

We must be careful to recognize that ideal types are used for empirical sense-making only. They do not reflect, authentically, the real life event. They only approximate the extent to which no one person or behavior is perfect.

# APPENDIX B:
# SURVEY INSTRUMENTS

Although questionnaires are typically self-administered survey forms that consist of a set of questions, for safety belt wearing surveys they are usually managed by a researcher. The field worker reads the questionnaire items to the respondents and marks in the answer. The responses can be structured into "forced" choices or they can be free unstructured.

Found in this appendix are the instruments which were used to gather data for certain studies. The forms follow the descriptions found in the methodologies.

# DRIVER SAFETY BELT USE

# INTERVIEW QUESTIONNAIRE
## SUMMER—FALL, 1986

1. What kind of car do you drive?

2. What year is your car?

3. How long have you been driving?

4. Roughly how much time, on an average day, do you spend in your car?
   - less than one hour
   - one to two hours
   - greater than two hours

5. Do you drive mainly on the highway, on city streets or on country dirt roads?

6. Do you consider yourself a cautious driver?

   [If yes] 6a. Why?

   [If no] 6b. Why not?

7. Do you consider yourself a regular safety belt wearer?

[If yes] 7a. Probably nobody wears safety belts all the time. What are some of the times when you don't wear them?

[If no] 7b. There are probably some times when you do wear safety belts. What are some of these times?

8. Do you think people who are caught not wearing safety belts should pay a fine?

[If yes] 8a. How much do you think the fine should be?

[If no] 8b. Do you think fines will get people to buckle up?

[If yes] 8c. Why?

9. Do you favor the compulsory use of safety belts?

[If yes] 9a. Why?

[If no] 9b. Why not?

10. What do you think most people think about wearing safety belts?

10a. Do you feel this way too?

[If yes or no] 10b. Why?

11. What are your impressions of people who never wear safety belts?

12. What are your impressions of people who always wear safety belts?

13. What do you think the chances are of being caught by the police for not wearing safety belts?

    _____ extremely high

    _____ moderately high

    _____ no opinion

    _____ moderately low

    _____ extremely low

14. Do you think that motorcycle riders who do not wear a helmet should pay a fine?

    [If yes] 14a. Why?

    [If no] 14b. Why not?

15. All the new cars have a high-mounted third brakelight. Research has shown that this reduces rear-end collisions. Do you think that all cars, even old ones, should be required to have these lights installed?

    [If yes] 15a. Why?

    [If no] 15b. Why not?

16. These days, a lot of people drive with their headlights on during the day. Are you one of these people?

[If yes] 16a. Why?

[If no] 16b. Why not?

17. How do you think most people feel about traffic police?

17a. Do you feel this way too?

[If yes or no] 17b. Why?

18. Do you think that current advertising programs are effective in reducing the number of people who drive while impaired?

[If yes or no] 18a. Why?

19. What kind of advertising program do you think may be effective for reducing the number of people who drive while impaired?

20. What is your present marital status?

    _____ Married

    _____ Single

    _____ Divorced

    _____ Separated

    _____ Widowed

21. What is your age?

22. What is your approximate annual income?

    _____ Less than 10,000

    _____ 10,000 – 19,999

    _____ 20,000 – 29,999

    _____ 30,000 – 39,999

    _____ 40,000 – 49,999

    _____ More than 50,000

23. Gender (observer noted)

# PROVINCIAL SAFETY
# BELT CAMPAIGN

# INTERVIEW QUESTIONNAIRE
# SUMMER — FALL, 1987

| INTERVIEWER . . . | JURISDICTION . . . | WEATHER . . . D W | B.C. Research |
| DAY . . . . . . . . . . . | SITE . . . . . . . . . . . | REFUSAL? . . Y | 2-01-307 |
| DATE – SEPT | NUMBER . . . . . . . . | 1 2 3 4 5 6 7 8 9+ | 87-08-11 |
| TIME   M   A   E | | NO. OF OCCUPANTS? | |

1. About how far have you driven since you last got into the car?     km ☐☐

2. Was any highway driving involved? . . Y   N
   IF YES,                                    less than half . . . 1
                                                 about half . . . 2
                                              more than half . . . 3

3. About how long have you been driving in B.C. (years)? ☐☐   And in total years? ☐☐

**IF DRIVER NOT WEARING**

4. Do you ever wear a seat belt?
   hardly ever or never . . . 1
   less than half the time . . . 2
   about half the time . . . 3
   more than half the time . . . 4

   a) If HARDLY EVER OR NEVER: Why is that? (Main reason)
   _____ ☐☐

   b) If YES: What is the main reason you are not wearing a seat belt at the moment?
   _____ ☐☐

**IF DRIVER WEARING**

5. How often do you wear a seat belt?
   less than half the time . . . 1
   about half the time . . . 2
   more than half the time . . . 3
   always . . . 4

   a) If NOT ALWAYS: What is the main reason you are wearing a seat belt at the moment?
   _____ ☐☐

   b) If ALWAYS: What is the main reason you always wear a seat belt?
   _____ ☐☐

IF THERE IS A CHILD OR CONVERTIBLE SEAT IN THE CAR

6. Is the back of your child seat attached to the car with a separate strap?   Y   N   N/A

IF THE VEHICLE IS A CAR

7. Have you had a rear-centre, high-mounted brake light installed?   Y   N   FI   N/A

8. Do you ever use your lights when driving in daylight?           Y   N   _____
   Under what conditions do you use them?                              _____

9. Do you think that campaigns should be conducted to increase safety belt usage?   Y   N   D   U
   If YES, who should be responsible for mounting these campaigns?

   _____ ☐☐     _____ ☐☐
   _____            _____

9287

| | LEFT | CENTRE | RIGHT |
|---|---|---|---|
| **F R O N T** | A. 0 1 2+ ?<br>Occupants | A. 0 1 2+ ?<br>Occupants | A. 0 1 2+ ?<br>Occupants |
| | B. M F ? | B. M F ? | B. M F ? |
| | C. <21 [ ] 22+ 25+ 40+ 55+ 70+ ? | C. <21 [ ] 22+ 25+ 40+ 55+ 70+ ? | C. <21 [ ] 22+ 25+ 40+ 55+ 70+ ? |
| | D. N L S I Co Ch B ?<br>1 2 3 4 5 6 7 | D. N L S I Co Ch B ?<br>1 2 3 4 5 6 7 | D. N L S I Co Ch B ?<br>1 2 3 4 5 6 7 |
| **R E A R** | A. 0 1 2+ ?<br>Occupants | A. 0 1 2+ ?<br>Occupants | A. 0 1 2+ ?<br>Occupants |
| | B. M F ? | B. M F ? | B. M F ? |
| | C. <21 [ ] 22+ 25+ 40+ 55+ 70+ ? | C. <21 [ ] 22+ 25+ 40+ 55+ 70+ ? | C. <21 [ ] 22+ 25+ 40+ 55+ 70+ ? |
| | D. N L S I Co Ch B ?<br>1 2 3 4 5 6 7 | D. N L S I Co Ch B ?<br>1 2 3 4 5 6 7 | D. N/ L S I Co Ch B ?<br>1 2 3 4 5 6 7 |
| **S U P P L E M E N T** | A. 0 1 2+ ?<br>Occupants | A. 0 1 2+ ?<br>Occupants | A. 0 1 2+ ?<br>Occupants |
| | B. M F ? | B. M F ? | B. M F ? |
| | C. <21 [ ] 22+ 25+ 40+ 55+ 70+ ? | C. <21 [ ] 22+ 25+ 40+ 55+ 70+ ? | C. <21 [ ] 22+ 25+ 40+ 55+ 70+ ? |
| | D. N L S I Co Ch B ?<br>1 2 3 4 5 6 7 | Ask #6<br>D. N L S I Co Ch B ?<br>1 2 3 4 5 6 7 | D. N L S I Co Ch B ?<br>1 2 3 4 5 6 7 |